Diet recommendations after burns

Please check these recommendations always with a nutrition consultant, therapist, doctor or dietician. The recipes and the list of ingredients are supporting the conventional medical therapy.
The calorie disclosures of fresh ingredients (fruit and vegetables) vary according to quality and time of harvest. The contents were checked by a dietician and a nutrition consultant for the Traditional Chinese Medicine (TCM).

Author:
©2017 Josef Miligui
www.ebns.at

AF285329

Source:
The lists are created from the EBNS database for nutritional counseling. The database is used by dietitians, therapists and doctors for advising the patient / client.

Literature:
The specialist literature and the training documents of the German and Austrian dietary and traditional Chinese medicine serve as a knowledge base. We have used the documents as a basis of knowledge, adapted it to our experience and completed them.
http://di-book.com

Title Photo:
©2008 Erika Weixlbaumer

Production and publishing:
BoD – Books on Demand, Norderstedt
ISBN: 9783752829334

Diet recommendations for DIETETICS - Changed nutrient requirements - after burns

1 Treatment strategy

Start with total parenteral nutrition (acute shock phase)
Stepwise transition to high caloric nutrition, depending on swallowing, appetite and tolerance of oral nutrition
Easily digestible food in a suitable consistency
Plenty of fluid
Increase calories (35-45 kcal / kg body weight)
protein requirement increased - high-protein supplement (2-3 g per kg body weight)
Frequently eat small meals (energy- and egg-rich intermediate meals!)
vitamin substitution

2 Avoid

Foods and herbs, which avoid urinating, in order to avoid water loss.

3 Breakfast

	kkal. per serving
Bean paste piquant sweet	311
Beef salad	249
Breakfast with cheese	593
Broccoli and Parmesan spread on toast bread	148
Bulgur with tomatoes and fresh herbs	205
Cottage cheese with steamed fruit	214
Cream cheese substitute	526
Curdcheesedumplings on strawberry pulp	553
Fish soup with rosemary	271

4 Snack

5 Lunch

6 Afternoon

7 Dinner

8   Any time

9 Recipes

(recommendable) = You can use more.
(little) = You should use less than specified or omit.

9.1 Andalusian fish pot

Strengthens immune system, prevents cancer, dissolves stagnation, promotes weight loss. Good to fight immunodeficiency, loss of appetite, flatulence, high blood pressure, depressions, diabetes, diarrhea, stimulates appetite.
Cooking time approx. 30 min
Calories p. portion: 348
4 portions
Allergens: ADLO

Quantity of ingredients:
Basic recipe for a vegetable soup (nutritious) 2 cups / 500g. (yes)
Onion (spring onion) 2 pieces / 40g. (yes)
Olive oil 1 table spoon / 20g. (recommended)
Lemon peel 1/2 piece / 3g. (yes)
Bay leaf 1 piece / 1g. (yes)
Potato 5/8 oz / 200g. (yes)
Cod 3/4 lbs / 300g. (yes)
White wine 4 table spoons / 80g. (yes)
Lemon juice 1/2 teaspoon / 10g. (yes)
Salt 1 pinch / 1g. (yes)
Pepper (ground) 1 pinch / 0,2g. (yes)
Parsley 1 table spoon / 15g. (yes)
White bread (wheat bread) 8 slices / 250g. (yes)

Cooking instructions:
Boil the vegetable broth with small spring onion, olive oil, grated lemon peel and bay leaf. Boil covered for 10 minutes. Add the peeled, diced potatoes and boil in about 8 minutes. Add fish pieces and white wine and switch to small heat. In the slightly boiling broth put the fish and boil it a few minutes. Season with lemon juice, salt and pepper. Serve with parsley sprinkled.
White bread as a side dish.

9.2 Basic recipe for a beef broth (clear)

Strengthens muscles, tendons and bones, reduces blood pressure, strengthens immune system, prevents cancer, reduces radiation damage, stimulates digestion, reduces pain, promotes digestion, diuretic. Rosemary stimulates digestion.
Cooking time approx. 4-8 hours
Calories p. portion: 114
10 portions
Allergens: O

Quantity of ingredients:
Beef soup meat 1,1 lbs / 500g. (yes)
Beef meatbones 5/8 oz / 200g. (yes)
Vinegar (Red wine vinegar) 1 dash / 3g. (yes)
Juniper berry 8 pieces / 6g. (yes)
Rosemary 1 pinch / 1g. (yes)
Carrot 3 pieces / 210g. (yes)
Parsnip 2 pieces / 300g. (yes)
Leek 1 piece / 200g. (yes)
Ginger fresh 1/2 teaspoon / 5g. (yes)
Lovage 1 stem / 15g. (yes)
Clove 2 pieces / 2g. (yes)
Pimento 6 pieces / 12g. (yes)
Anise (Common Fennel) 2 pieces / 1g. (yes)
Salt 1 teaspoon / 5g. (yes)
Water 3,3 lbs / 1300g. (yes)

Cooking instructions:
Heat water, a dash of red wine vinegar, some juniper berries, a little rosemary, bones and meat till it boils; add carrot, parsnip, leek, ginger, lovage, clove, allspice, star anise and a little salt; simmer for 4-8 hours then strain. Refrigerate for later use.

9.3 Basic recipe for a chicken broth worming

Strengthens blood, strengthens bone marrow, reduces blood pressure, strengthens immune system, prevents cancer, reduces radiation damage, promotes sweating, dissolves stagnation, good to fight loss of appetite, flatulence.
Cooking time approx. 2-3 hours
Calories p. portion: 90
9 portions
Allergens: L

Quantity of ingredients:
Chicken meat 1/2 piece / 600g. (yes)
Carrot 2 pieces / 150g. (yes)
Leek 1 stick / 45g. (yes)
Celery root 1 piece / 500g. (yes)
Ginger fresh 2 slices / 2g. (yes)
Fenugreek (Trigonella foenum-graecum) 1 teaspoon / 2g. (yes)
Juniper berry 1 teaspoon / 3g. (yes)
Bay leaf 3 pieces / 2g. (yes)
Water 4 cup / 900g. (yes)

Cooking instructions:
Remove chicken parts from fat. Place chicken pieces in a saucepan with hot water and heat till it boils briefly, skimming any resulting foam. Add coarsely chopped vegetables and all spices and cook over medium heat for 2 to 3 hours. Strain the finished soup. Throw away vegetables and bones.
Tip: If you want to use the meat as a soup insert, take out after 45 minutes and return only the bones in the soup.
Refrigerate for later use.

9.4   Basic recipe for a duck broth

Forcing spleen, strengthens blood, supports urination, reduces blood pressure, strengthens immune system, prevents cancer, reduces radiation damage.
Cooking time approx. 2-3 hours
Calories p. portion: 61
6 portions
Allergens: L

Quantity of ingredients:
Water 2 cup / 450g. (yes)
Duck (heart) 5/8 oz / 200g. (yes)
Duck (slaughtered) 1/4 lbs - 4oz / 100g. (recommended)
Carrot 2 pieces / 100g. (yes)
Celery root 1/2 piece / 600g. (yes)

Cooking instructions:
Cook duck pieces with vegetables for 2-3 hours. Sift broth through a fine sieve and refrigerate for later use.
The innards can be reused: You cut them finely and leaves them for a

few minutes with fresh vegetables in the broth draw. Sprinkle with parsley before serving.

9.5   Basic recipe for a fish broth

Strengthens the kidneys, promotes watering, reduces blood pressure, strengthens immune system, prevents cancer, reduces radiation damage. Low in cholesterol and protein rich. Improves blood circulation, stimulates appetite.
Cooking time approx. 40 min
Calories p. portion: 128
5 portions
Allergens: DLO

Quantity of ingredients:
Fish pieces mixed (fresh water) 3/4 lbs / 300g. (yes)
Celery root 1/4 lbs - 4oz / 120g. (yes)
Leek 2 inches / 10g. (yes)
Carrot 2 pieces / 150g. (yes)
White wine 1/2 cup / 125g. (yes)
Lemon 1/2 piece / 50g. (yes)
Bay leaf 2 leaves / 2g. (yes)
Peppercorns 3 pieces / 2g. (yes)
Olive oil 1 table spoon / 10g. (recommended)
Water 2 cup / 450g. (yes)

Cooking instructions:
Fry celery, chopped carrots and leeks in olive oil, add bay leaf and peppercorns, add pieces of fish and sauté briefly. Add water, add little white wine or lemon. Simmer gently for 30 minutes. Skim off the resulting foam several times. In the end, sift the ingredients through a cloth.
Refrigerate for later use

9.6   Basic recipe for a vegetable soup, nutritious

Reduces blood pressure, strengthens immune system, prevents cancer, forcing spleen, dissolves stagnation, promotes weight loss. Good to fight immunodeficiency, high blood pressure, depressions, diabetes, diarrhea, reduces blood lipids.
Cooking time approx. 2-3 hours
Calories p. portion: 48
5 portions
Allergens: L

Quantity of ingredients:
Olive oil 1 table spoon / 4g. (recommended)
Onion white 1 piece / 60g. (yes)
Carrot 3 pieces / 200g. (yes)
Parsnip 3/8 lbs - 6oz / 150g. (yes)
Celery root 1 cup / 100g. (yes)
Ginger fresh 1/2 teaspoon / 2g. (yes)
Lemon 1/2 piece / 25g. (yes)
Juniper berry 6 pieces / 6g. (yes)
Thyme dried 1 pinch / 1g. (yes)
Lovage 1 table spoon / 3g. (yes)
Bay leaf 2 leaves / 1g. (yes)
Salt 1 pinch / 1g. (yes)
Water 3 cups / 650g. (yes)

Cooking instructions:
Cut the vegetables into cubes.
Heat oil in hot pot, fry shortly onions and vegetables.
Add cold water, then add ginger, bay leaf and lemon juice.
Season with juniper, thyme and lovage. Cover for 2 - 3 hours on a low heat and simmer.
The used vegetables should be thrown away.
The basic recipe serves as a soup base and to refine vegetables, legumes or cereals.
If you want to eat vegetable soup immediately, add the desired vegetables half an hour before.
Refrigerate for later use.

9.7   Bean paste piquant sweet

Supports urination, lowers cholesterol, prevents arteriosclerosis, antioxidativ. Promotes digestion, helps to digest fat, supports urination, reduces blood pressure.
Cooking time approx. 1 hour
Calories p. portion: 311
1 portions
Allergens: MO

Quantity of ingredients:
Black beans 1 cup / 120g. (yes)
Ginger fresh 1 inch / 3g. (yes)
Boxhorn clover seeds 1/2 teaspoon / 2g. (yes)

Tomato paste 1 table spoon / 10g. (yes)
Olive oil 2 table spoons / 20g. (recommended)
Pumpkin seed oil 1 dash / 3g. (recommended)
Mustard 1 knife tip / 1g. (yes)
Radish horseradish 1 teaspoon (grated) / 2g. (yes)
Pepper (ground) 1 pinch / 0,5g. (yes)
Garlic 2 cloves / 3g. (yes)
Salt 1 pinch / 1g. (yes)
Sugar molasses 2 table spoons / 20g. (recommended)
Lemon peel 1/2 piece / 1g. (yes)

Cooking instructions:
Boil beans (with spices and ginger), drain water and puree. Season with spices.

Refine with sugar beet syrup and lemon peel.

9.8 Beef pumpkin and vegetable stew

Reduces inflammation, improves digestion, reduces blood glucose, strengthens the muscles, tendons and bones, promotes digestion, helps to digest fat.
Cooking time approx. 1 hour
Calories p. portion: 369
4 portions
Allergens: AL

Quantity of ingredients:
Beef meat 3/4 lbs / 350g. (yes)
Pumpkin 3/4 lbs / 350g. (yes)
Leek 3/8 lbs - 6oz / 150g. (yes)
Potato 3/4 lbs / 350g. (yes)
Tomato 3/8 lbs - 6oz / 150g. (yes)
Olive oil 2 table spoons / 25g. (recommended)
Basic recipe for a vegetable soup 1/4 lbs - 4oz / 125g. (yes)
Salt 1 pinch / 1g. (yes)
Pepper (ground) 1 pinch / 0,5g. (yes)
Peppers powder 1 teaspoon / 2g. (yes)
Ground caraway 1 pinch / 1g. (yes)
Sugar cane sugar 1 pinch / 1g. (recommended)
Parsley 1/2 bunch / 30g. (yes)
White bread (wheat bread) 4 slices / 80g. (yes)

Cooking instructions:
Dice beef. Peel pumpkin and dice. Cut the leek into rings and dice the peeled potatoes.
Brew the tomatoes with boiling water, peel off the skin and dice.
Steam the meat in olive oil and fill with vegetable stock. Add the cleaned vegetables. Season with salt, pepper, paprika, cumin and fructose.
Stew for 30 minutes over low heat.
Season again and sprinkle with parsley and serve with white bread.

9.9   Beef salad

Strengths spleen and stomach, strengthens blood, strengthens the muscles, tendons and bones, diuretic, detoxifying, suppresses conversion of sugar into fat, lowers cholesterol, dissolves stagnation.
Cooking time approx. 10 min
Calories p. portion: 249
1 portions
Allergens: O

Quantity of ingredients:
Beef meat 1/8 lbs - 2oz / 50g. (yes)
Onion white 1/2 oz / 20g. (yes)
Peppers 1 oz / 30g. (yes)
Cucumber (spicy cucumber) 1 oz / 30g. (yes)
Vinegar (Apple vinegar) 2 teaspoons / 5g. (yes)
Rapeseed oil 2 teaspoons / 5g. (recommended)
Salt 1 pinch / 0,5g. (yes)
Pepper (ground) 1 pinch / 0,1g. (yes)
Chives 1 table spoon / 7g. (yes)
Bread with carob kernel flour 2 slices / 50g. (yes)

Cooking instructions:
Cook the meat with the basic recipe of a beef broth and let it cool down. Cut into 1 cm slices. Cut the onions into rings, pepper and gherkin into small cubes. Mix all ingredients. Make the salad marinade with vinegar, oil and salt and pour over, season to taste and strain.

9.10 Beef with red wine

Strengths spleen and stomach, strengthens blood, strengthens the muscles, tendons and bones. For strengthening after diseases, mood brightening, good to fight cardiovascular disorders and fullness.
Promotes digestion, diuretic.
Cooking time approx. 2 hours and more
Calories p. portion: 202
4 portions
Allergens: O

Quantity of ingredients:
Beef fillet 1 lbs / 500g. (yes)
Red wine 1 cup / 250g. (yes)
Star anise 3 pieces / 2g. (yes)
Juniper berry 1 teaspoon / 2g. (yes)
Apricots 6 pieces (dried) / 50g. (yes)
Salt 1 pinch / 0,5g. (yes)
Water 1 cup / 200g. (yes)

Cooking instructions:
Cut beef into small pieces, sprinkle with red wine. Add star anise, finely crush juniper. Halve the apricots and add. Marinate for 2 hours. Put in a saucepan, salt and simmer for 1 hour. If necessary, add some water.

9.11 Braised rabbit with rice and lettuce

Improves blood circulation, stimulates appetite.
Cooking time approx. 1 hour
Calories p. portion: 522
6 portions
Allergens: LMO

Quantity of ingredients:
Olive oil 2 table spoons / 20g. (recommended)
Rabbit meat 1 piece (in 10-12 pieces) / 1200g. (yes)
Olive oil 2 table spoons / 20g. (recommended)
Carrot 2 pieces / 180g. (yes)
Garlic 2 cloves / 3g. (yes)
Celery sticks 1 stick / 10g. (yes)
Onion white 1 piece / 60g. (yes)
White wine 1 1/2 cups / 250g. (yes)
Water 1/2 cup / 0g. (yes)
Water 6 cups / 400g. (yes)

Rice Basmati 1 cup / 120g. (yes)
Salt 1 pinch / 1g. (yes)
Lamb's lettuce 3/4 lbs / 300g. (yes)
Olive oil 2 table spoons / 20g. (recommended)
Lemon juice 1/4 piece / 8g. (yes)
Mustard 1 pinch / 1g. (yes)
Salt 1 pinch / 1g. (yes)
Honey 1 pinch / 1g. (yes)

Cooking instructions:
In a heavy pan, heat the oil at low temperature. Add the rabbit parts, fry vigorously all around and then place on a plate.
Heat the oil in the pan, add the carrot, garlic, celery and onion, fry until golden brown while stirring several times and push aside.
Put the rabbit parts back into the pan, spread the vegetables over them and then pour in the wine and simmer for a few moments.
Pour in the water and heat till it boils. Put on the lid, reduce the heat supply and check in between times if there is enough liquid left. Add salt and simmer the rabbit for at least 90 minutes or until the meat is tender.

In the meantime, cook the rice in a saucepan with six times of salted water, on a low heat.

Wash the lettuce, finch and pt in a bowl. In a small bowl, mix the olive oil, lemon juice, mustard, salt and honey well and add to the salad and mix.

9.12 Breakfast with cheese

Good to fight weakness, stomach pressure, belching, diabetes, acute or chronic obstruction of the bowel, skin problems. Coffee supports urinating, stimulates appetite, detoxifying, increases blood glucose levels, harmonizes heart rhythm.
Cooking time approx. 10 min
Calories p. portion: 593
1 portions
Allergens: AGO

Quantity of ingredients:
Water 1 cup / 120g. (yes)
Coffee 2 teaspoons / 4g. (yes)
Whole grain bread 2 slices / 100g. (yes)
Margarine 1/2 oz / 10g. (recommended)

Edam cheese 1 oz / 30g. (yes)
Strawberry jam 1/2 oz / 20g. (yes)
Curd cheese 20% 1/8 lbs - 2oz / 40g. (yes)

Cooking instructions:
Prepare coffee as usual. Avoid sugar or use sweetener. Cover the bread slices with margarine and put the cheese and marmalade on the breakfast table. Decorating decoratively increases your appetite.

9.13 Broccoli and Parmesan spread on toast bread

Good to fight loss of appetite, blood clotting, thyroid function, increase Vitamin B12, strengthen immune system, good to fight belching, diabetes, acute or chronic constipation, dissolves stagnation.
Cooking time approx. 15 min
Calories p. portion: 148
2 portions
Allergens: AG

Quantity of ingredients:
Broccoli 5/8 oz / 200g. (yes)
Curd cheese 20% 3 oz / 80g. (yes)
Yogurt (natural, 1.5% fat) 1 table spoon / 10g. (yes)
Parmesan 2 table spoons / 15g. (recommended)
Lemon peel 1/2 teaspoon / 1g. (yes)
Basil (fresh) 1 table spoon / 5g. (yes)
Chives 1 table spoon / 5g. (yes)
Salt 1 pinch / 1g. (yes)
Pepper (ground) 1 pinch / 0,3g. (yes)
Toast bread (whole grain) 6 slices / 24g. (yes)

Cooking instructions:
Cook broccoli in a sieve insert over steam for 8 minutes until firm. Finely chop broccoli.
Mix the curd, yoghurt, parmesan and lemon peel well. Mix cheese cream with broccoli, basil and chives. Season the spread with salt and pepper. Serve on the crunchy toasted toast.

9.14 Bulgur with tomatoes and fresh herbs

Promotes digestion, helps to digest fat, supports urination, reduces blood pressure. Stimulates digestion, supports urination.
Cooking time approx. 30 min
Calories p. portion: 205
1 portions
Allergens: A

Quantity of ingredients:
Bulgur (cereals) 1 cup / 120g. (yes)
Tomato 2 pieces / 70g. (yes)
Rucola 2 table spoons / 16g. (yes)
Pepper powder (hot) 1 pinch / 2g. (yes)
Olive oil 2 table spoons / 20g. (recommended)
Pepper (ground) 1 pinch / 0,5g. (yes)
Salt 1 pinch / 1g. (yes)
Basil 4 leaves / 2g. (yes)
Thyme 1 Twig / 3g. (yes)
Lemon juice 1/2 piece / 10g. (yes)

Cooking instructions:
Put cold water in a pot, sprinkle in Bulgur and simmer. Stir in chopped tomatoes, fresh herbs like basil, thyme, arugula, a pinch of rose paprika, lemon juice, a dash of olive oil, a little ground pepper, some salt.

Variant: add some mozzarella.

Recommendation: ideal morning meal in summer; also suitable as evening meal, especially for sleep disorders.

9.15 Carp soup

Increase milk production and sweating, dissolves stagnation, reduces blood pressure, strengthens immune system, improves blood circulation, improves medication effect, stimulates appetite. Strengthens gastrointestinal function, expands blood vessels.
Cooking time approx. 2 hours
Calories p. portion: 499
2 portions
Allergens: DO

Quantity of ingredients:
Carp 1,1 lbs / 500g. (yes)
Salt 1 pinch / 1g. (yes)
Vinegar (Apple vinegar) 1 teaspoon / 3g. (yes)
Thyme 1 Twig / 3g. (yes)
Juniper berry 8 pieces / 3g. (yes)
Carrot 2 pieces / 200g. (yes)
Leek 1 piece / 200g. (yes)
Onion white 1 piece / 60g. (yes)
Ginger fresh 1/2 teaspoon / 2g. (yes)
Bay leaf 3 leaves / 1g. (yes)
White wine 1/2 cup / 125g. (yes)
Basil 3 leaves / 1g. (yes)

Cooking instructions:
Preparation: When shopping at the fishmonger, remove the fillets from a medium-sized, whole carp and also pack the fish head, spine with bones and tail.

Cut the fillets into 1 cm cubes; salt and set aside.

Place fish head, backbone and tail of carp in plenty of cold water; heat till it boils and scoop the foam; add a dash of vinegar, a fresh sprig of thyme, juniper berries; Add carrot, a piece of leek and chopped onion; add a thick slice of ginger, some peppercorns, 1 bay leaf, salt; simmer for about 1 1/2 hours and pour the stock through a sieve.

Put the carp pieces in a saucepan; pour a shot of white wine; Add rose paprika, basil leaves, finely ground carrots, dried thyme and the stock and warm; Boil the ingredients for about 5 minutes until the fish pieces are cooked.
Variants: Thicken the soup with kudzu or mashed potatoes.
This fits: baguette and dry white wine.

9.16 Chicken in an ilalian style

Strengthens bone marrow, improves blood circulation, strengthens the muscles, antioxidativ. Basmati rice: To drain the body overweight and high blood pressure.
Cooking time approx. 1 hour
Calories p. portion: 410
4 portions
Allergens: M

Quantity of ingredients:
Olive oil 2 table spoons / 30g. (recommended)
Chicken meat 1 piece (cut into 8 pieces) / 700g. (yes)
Garlic 3 cloves / 5g. (yes)
Rosemary 1/2 teaspoon / 2g. (yes)
Salt 1 pinch / 1g. (yes)
Pepper (ground) 1 pinch / 0,5g. (yes)
Water 1 cup / 20g. (yes)
Rice Basmati 1 cup / 120g. (yes)
Water 6 cups / 400g. (yes)
Salt 1 pinch / 1g. (yes)
Lettuce 1 piece / 300g. (yes)
Olive oil 2 table spoons / 20g. (recommended)
Lemon juice 1/4 piece / 7g. (yes)
Mustard 1 pinch / 3g. (yes)
Salt 1 pinch / 1g. (yes)
Honey 1 pinch / 2g. (yes)

Cooking instructions:
In a heavy pan (with lid) heat 1 tbsp of olive oil at low temperature. Add the chicken pieces and fry for a few minutes. Once they start to take on color, add the remaining 2 tablespoons of olive oil and garlic. Turn the chicken parts in the oil and sprinkle with rosemary, salt and pepper. Pour with a little water and heat till it boils. Reduce the heat, put on the lid and stew the chicken for 35 to 45 minutes.

In between, check again and again whether there is enough cooking water, and if necessary, add 1 to 2 tablespoons of water each time.

As soon as the meat comes off the bone, spread the chicken parts on the plates, deglaze the roast residue in the braised pan with a few tablespoons of water or wine and spread over the meat as a sauce.

In the meantime, cook the rice in a saucepan with (1:6) salted water, on a low heat.

Wash and spin the lettuce, finely chop and serve in a bowl. In a small bowl, mix the olive oil, lemon juice, mustard, salt and honey well and add to the salad and add it to the salad.

9.17 Chicken with white turnips on rice

Strengthens bone marrow. Rice to drain the body at overweight and high blood pressure.
Cooking time approx. 45 min
Calories p. portion: 324
4 portions
Allergens: GL

Quantity of ingredients:
Butter organic 2 table spoons / 20g. (recommended)
Olive oil 2 table spoons / 20g. (recommended)
Onion white 1 piece / 60g. (yes)
Turnips 4 pieces / 200g. (yes)
Garlic 2 pieces / 3g. (yes)
Basic recipe for a chicken soup (warming) 1 cup / 100g. (yes)
Parsley 2 table spoons / 15g. (yes)
Salt 1 pinch / 1g. (yes)
Olive oil 1 teaspoon / 4g. (recommended)
Chicken meat 7/8 lbs / 400g. (yes)
Water 6 cups / 400g. (yes)
Rice Basmati 1 cup / 120g. (yes)

Cooking instructions:
In a heavy pot, heat the butter and the oil at low temperature. Add the onion, stir and simmer for about 20 minutes on very low heat until soft and golden brown. Add the chopped beets and the chopped garlic cloves and stir well. Add the chicken broth or water, add some salt and heat till it boils. Reduce the heat, put on the lid and simmer the beets for about 20 minutes. Look in between if there is still enough liquid in the pot, and if necessary, pour in a few tablespoons of chicken stock. At the end there should be very little liquid in the pot. Remove the lid and allow the remaining liquid to evaporate, stirring constantly.
In the meantime roast the finely chopped chicken pieces in a frying pan with a little oil. Finally, sprinkle with a little chili and fry for another minute while constantly turning.
Serve the pieces of chicken, turnips and rice on the plates, spread the sauce over them and sprinkle with parsley immediately.
Cook the rice in the ratio of 6 cups of water: 1 cup of rice.
Small, fresh, untreated beets do not need to be peeled. Otherwise, peel beets and place in hot water for 10 minutes. This makes them easier to digest and lose some of their sharp, pungent odor. White turnips are rich in vitamin C, potassium and folic acid.

9.18 Classic ginger chicken with rice wine

Forcing spleen, blood and bone marrow. Relieves fatigue, regulates gastrointestinal function. Diuretic, building up, eye-enhancing, detoxifying, nerve-strengthening.
Cooking time approx. 30 min
Calories p. portion: 357
4 portions
Allergens: GO

Quantity of ingredients:
Butter organic 2 table spoons / 30g. (recommended)
Ginger fresh 2 table spoons / 18g. (yes)
Salt 1 pinch / 0,5g. (yes)
Chicken meat 2 pieces (legs) / 500g. (yes)
Lychee liqueur 1 dash / 2g. (yes)
Curry 1 pinch / 1g. (yes)
Sake 1 dash / 1g. (yes)
Corn 4 table spoons / 30g. (yes)
Millet 1/2 cup / 50g. (yes)
Salt 1 pinch / g. (yes)
Water 1 1/2 cups / 200g. (yes)
Lettuce 1/2 piece / 100g. (yes)
Olive oil 1 table spoon / 10g. (recommended)
Vinegar (Apple vinegar) 1 teaspoon / 3g. (yes)
Water 2 table spoons / 20g. (yes)
Salt 1 pinch / 0,5g. (yes)
Herbs various 1 table spoon / 8g. (yes)

Cooking instructions:
Heat butter in a hot pan (preferably made of cast iron or enamel); sauté chopped ginger (about 1 heaped tablespoons per chicken leg) on low heat; add some salt, chicken and/or other parts of the chicken and roast all around with gentle heat; add Lychee liqueur or maple syrup, add a little curry and fry for a short time; stir in plenty of sake; add corn kernels (from the glass, health food trade); boil all the ingredients in the sauce for a few minutes, until the meat is cooked; season with salt.

This fits: millet, lettuce or lettuce.

9.19 Clear soup from goose

Promotes sweating, dissolves stagnation. Reduces blood pressure, strengthens immune system, expands blood vessels, stimulates digestion, reduces pain.
Cooking time approx. 2-3 hours
Calories p. portion: 334
6 portions
Allergens:

Quantity of ingredients:
Goose parts 1,1 lbs / 500g. (recommended)
Carrot 1 piece / 100g. (yes)
Onion (shallot) 1 piece / 25g. (yes)
Leek 1 piece / 250g. (yes)
Parsley 1 Twig / 4g. (yes)
Lovage 1 Twig / 4g. (yes)
Chervil 1 pinch / 0,2g. (yes)
Water 4 cup / 1000g. (yes)
Salt 1 pinch / 0,5g. (yes)

Cooking instructions:
Simmer goose pieces with vegetables and herbs for 2-3 hours. Sift through a fine cloth and cool. Degrease and store in the refrigerator.

9.20 Cottage cheese with steamed fruit

Good to fight loss of appetite, promotes digestion, supports urination.
Cooking time approx. 20 min
Calories p. portion: 214
2 portions
Allergens: G

Quantity of ingredients:
Cottage cheese 3/4 lbs / 300g. (yes)
Apple (sour) 1 piece / 100g. (yes)
Pear 1 piece / 100g. (yes)

Cooking instructions:
Wash apples and pears well, do not peel, and chop small. In a pot with steam filter, boil them al dente, remove and allow to cool down.
Serve the cheese, spread the fruit on it.

9.21 Cream cheese substitute

Good to fight lactose intolerance. Strengthens body energy, promotes digestion, promotes weight loss. Good to fight immunodeficiency, loss of appetite, arteriosclerosis, flatulence, bladder weakness, anemia, high blood pressure, depressions, diabetes, diarrhea.
Cooking time approx. 20 min
Calories p. portion: 526
2 portions
Allergens: AE

Quantity of ingredients:
Soybean milk 4 cup / 300g. (yes)
Lemon 1 piece / 50g. (yes)
Herbs various 2 table spoons / 6g. (yes)
Whole grain bread 6 slices / 300g. (yes)

Cooking instructions:
Heat the soy milk in a saucepan till it boils, stirring occasionally (gets burn easily!), Then allow to cool.
Squeeze out the lemon and stir gently under the cooled soy milk (approx. 80°C/176°F), let it approx. 20 min. rest or clot.
Pour chopped soy milk through a strainer lined with a dishcloth, allow liquid to drain and then squeeze out remaining liquid with the dishcloth.
Refine to taste with fresh herbs.
Serve with wholemeal bread.

9.22 Curdcheesedumplings on strawberry pulp

Strawberry forcing spleen and stomach, strengthens blood. Chicken egg calms nerves and stomach.
Cooking time approx. 30 min
Calories p. portion: 553
5 portions
Allergens: ACG

Quantity of ingredients:
Curd cheese 20% 1,1 lbs / 500g. (yes)
Spelled semolina 3/8 lbs - 6oz / 150g. (yes)
Butter organic 1/8 lbs - 2oz / 40g. (recommended)
Chicken egg 2 pieces / 120g. (yes)
Sugar - icing sugar 2 table spoons / 20g. (recommended)
Salt 1 pinch / 1g. (yes)
Breadcrumbs (wheat bread, bread roll) 2 table spoons / 25g. (yes)

Butter organic 1/4 lbs - 4oz / 100g. (recommended)
Strawberries 1,1 lbs / 500g. (yes)
Sugar - icing sugar 2 table spoons / 25g. (recommended)

Cooking instructions:
Curdcheese, grit, butter, eggs, powdered sugar and salt to a smooth
dough. Keep the dough 15 mins in the refrigerator to settle down. Then
shape small dumplings with a diameter of approx 4cm and boil them for
about 10 minutes in slightly boiling salt water. Heat butter in a pan and
roast the breadcrumbs golden brown. Roll the dumplings carefully into
the crumbs.
Serve the dumplings with the strawberry.

9.23 Duck soup with algae

Strengthens blood, forcing spleen, Supports urination. reduces blood
pressure, strengthens immune system, prevents cancer, reduces
radiation damage, detoxifying and stimulating the immune system.
Cooking time approx. 3-4 hours
Calories p. portion: 664
4 portions
Allergens: E

Quantity of ingredients:
Duck (slaughtered) 2 cup / 1000g. (recommended)
Garlic 2 cloves / 4g. (yes)
Onion white 1 piece / 50g. (yes)
Ginger fresh 1/2 teaspoon / 2g. (yes)
Curcuma 1/2 teaspoon / 2g. (yes)
Carrot 2 pieces / 120g. (yes)
Lemon 2 cup / 15g. (yes)
Cinnamon ground 1/4 stick / 3g. (yes)
Star anise 2 pieces / 2g. (yes)
Fish sauce 1 teaspoon / 3g. (yes)
Soy sauce 2 teaspoons / 6g. (yes)
Juniper berry 4 pieces / 2g. (yes)
Coriander (fresh) 1/4 Bunch / 100g. (yes)
Wakame 1/4 lbs / 100g. (yes)

Cooking instructions:
This soup tastes better, the next day.
1. Place the duck with its innards (with the exception of the liver), the
cleaned vegetables and all the spices (a little coriander leaves retained)

in a large saucepan and cover with water. Bring to the boil and simmer for about 2 hours.

2. Trigger the meat cleanly, parry the innards, and cut into accurate, bite-sized slices or cubes. Pour over some broth and set aside. Put the bones and skin back into the soup in the pot, cook everything for another 3 - 4 hours, until the vegetables begins to dissolve.

3. Degrease the soup, which works best if left cold overnight and the fat on the surface solidifies. Heat the soup again and drive through a sieve.

4. To serve, chop the algae and simmer for 5 minutes in the soup, add the meat and reheat.

5. Season the soup with fish sauce and lemon juice and sprinkle with the remaining cilantro.

9.24 Duck with mung beans

Strengthens blood, forcing spleen, supports urination, promotes spleen and liver, reduces blood pressure, strengthens immune system, prevents cancer, reduces radiation damage, dissolves stagnation.
Cooking time approx. 2 hours
Calories p. portion: 747
5 portions
Allergens: E

Quantity of ingredients:
Duck (slaughtered) 1/2 piece / 1250g. (recommended)
Onion white 2 pieces / 120g. (yes)
Carrot 1 piece / 120g. (yes)
Garlic 1 clove / 3g. (yes)
Mung bean 5/8 lbs - 8oz / 250g. (yes)
Peppercorns 3 pieces / 2g. (yes)
Honey 1 teaspoon / 3g. (yes)
Soy sauce 1 teaspoon / 3g. (yes)
Lemon juice 1 teaspoon / 3g. (yes)
Salt 1 pinch / 1g. (yes)
Pepper (ground) 1 pinch / 0,5g. (yes)
Olive oil 1 table spoon / 10g. (recommended)
Bay leaf 2 leaves / 2g. (yes)
Black caraway 1 pinch / 1g. (yes)
Savory 1 teaspoon / 2g. (yes)

Cooking instructions:
The day before soak the mung beans and rinse the duck cold. Wash the vegetables, clean and cut into pieces. Put the duck and vegetables in a saucepan and cover with water. Add bay leaves, savory, mugwort and peppercorns. Boil over medium heat and simmer for 45 minutes. Skim off the foam. Remove duck from the stock, allow to cool and keep cool overnight.

In a saucepan, sauté the chopped onion in olive oil and pour in 1/4 liter of stock and add the pre-cooked vegetables. Add the mung beans and season with honey, soy sauce, lemon juice, salt, crushed black cumin and pepper.

Serve with rice or potatoes.

9.25 Figs with mozzarella and honey

Promotes digestion, reduces inflammation, bloating and nausea, relaxing and reassuring, relieves pain, detoxifying, blood stilling, forcing spleen and digestive system, detoxifying, bactericide.
Cooking time approx. 10 min
Calories p. portion: 415
1 portions
Allergens: GO

Quantity of ingredients:
Fig 4 pieces / 100g. (yes)
Mozzarella 1 piece / 50g. (yes)
Basil (fresh) 1/2 bunch / 50g. (yes)
Honey 2 table spoons / 24g. (yes)
Pepper (ground) 1 pinch / 0,1g. (yes)
Grapeseed oil 1 table spoon / 12g. (yes)
Vinegar Aceto Balsamico white 1 table spoon / 12g. (yes)

Cooking instructions:
Quarter fresh figs, dice buffalo mozzarella, pluck basil leaves.
Mix a dressing with light balsamic vinegar, grapeseed oil and honey and season to taste.
Place the figs on the edge of the appropriate plate. Spread the mozzarella cubes and season with black pepper. Spread whole or roughly sliced basil leaves over it and moisten with the marinade.
Spiced pizza bread goes perfectly with it.

9.26 Fish soup with rosemary

Promotes spleen and liver, reduces blood pressure, strengthens immune system, prevents cancer, reduces radiation damage, has little cholesterol and is protein rich, improves blood circulation, increases appetite. Antioxidant, forcing spleen, dissolves stagnation.
Cooking time approx. 30 min
Calories p. portion: 271
4 portions
Allergens: DLO

Quantity of ingredients:
Basic recipe for a fish soup 2 cup / 500g. (yes)
Rosemary 1/2 bunch / 7g. (yes)
Onion (spring onion) 1 piece / 20g. (yes)
Olive oil 2 table spoons / 35g. (recommended)
Fish pieces mixed (fresh water) 5/8 lbs - 8oz / 250g. (yes)
Carrot 1 piece / 120g. (yes)
Parsnip 1 piece / 180g. (yes)
Celery root 1 slice / 20g. (yes)
Salt 1 pinch / 1g. (yes)
Peppercorns 2 pieces / 1g. (yes)
Garlic 1 clove / 3g. (yes)

Cooking instructions:
Fry the onion and garlic in oil. Add fish broth. Add diced carrots, parsnips and celery. Season with salt and peppercorns. Simmer the soup on a low heat for 25 minutes.
Wash the fish, drizzle with lemon juice, divide into pieces and add to the soup with the pink rosemary. Cook for 5 min on low heat.
Add the chives and parsley and season the soup with the salt.

9.27 Grilled salmon steaks with cauliflower and potatoes

Improves digestion, regenerates skin, supports urination, lowers cholesterol, supports digestion.
Cooking time approx. 30 min
Calories p. portion: 330
4 portions
Allergens: D

Quantity of ingredients:

Garlic 1 clove / 1g. (yes)
Onion (shallot) 1/2 piece / 5g. (yes)
Lemon juice 1 dash / 1g. (yes)
Salt 1 pinch / 1g. (yes)
Cauliflower 1 piece / 500g. (yes)
Olive oil 2 table spoons / 20g. (recommended)
Garlic 1 clove / 1g. (yes)
Water 2/3 cup / g. (yes)
Parsley 2 table spoons / 15g. (yes)
Potato 1,1 lbs / 500g. (yes)
Salt 1 pinch / 1g. (yes)
Salmon 4 pieces (steaks) / 500g. (recommended)
Lemon 1/2 piece / 2g. (yes)

Cooking instructions:

Garlic shallots mixture:
Finely squeeze the garlic, finely chop the shallots, add a dash of lemon juice and salt and stir. Mix with a little oil to a paste.

Cauliflower:
Cut the cauliflower into pieces.
Heat the oil in a heavy saucepan and fry the crushed garlic for a short time.
Add the cauliflower pieces and turn in the oil. Add a little water and cook until the cauliflower is firm. Strain the cauliflower and cook the remaining water until a thick sauce remains. Add the cauliflower and crush it roughly with a wooden spoon. Add the chopped parsley and salt.

Potatoes:
Cook the potato in a saucepan with plenty of water, strain and peel.

Salmon Steak:
Preheat the oven at about 180°C/356°F. Rub in the salmon slices with the garlic-scarlet mixture and grill as close as possible to the heat source for 4 to 8 minutes from both sides. You are done when the meat is easy to divide when you pierce with a fork.

Serve and sprinkle with lemon slices and the chopped parsley.

9.28 Grilled tofu with rice noodles, spinach and sugar snaps

Reduces flatulence. Supports urination, detoxifying. Good to fight blood circulation disorders. Strengthens gastrointestinal function, expands blood vessels, stimulates appetite. Promotes bowel movement, improves blood circulation.
Cooking time approx. 30 min
Calories p. portion: 327
4 portions
Allergens: E

Quantity of ingredients:
Sake 1/3 cup / 85g. (yes)
Sugar cane sugar 1 table spoon / 7g. (recommended)
Garlic 5 cloves / 7g. (yes)
Onion (spring onion) 3 pieces / 60g. (yes)
Ginger fresh 1 inch / 5g. (yes)
Rapeseed oil 2 table spoons / 20g. (recommended)
Spinach 2 handful / 30g. (yes)
Peas, green 7/8 lbs / 400g. (yes)
Water 1 table spoon / g. (yes)
Rice noodles 1 package / 250g. (yes)
Water 4 cup / g. (yes)
Basil 1 table spoon / 3g. (yes)
Soy Tofu 1,1 lbs / 500g. (yes)

Cooking instructions:
In a medium bowl mix together: Tamari souce, rice wine, sugar, crushed garlic, spring onion, grated ginger, chopped basil and the rapeseed oil. Add the tofu and leave in the marinade for at least 1 hour. Cover the mangetout peas in a pan with a little water, lightly simmer 5 min. Add the spinach and steam again 3 min.

Cook the rice noodles according to manufacturer's instructions, drain, rinse again with warm water and drain.
Preheat the grill or oven grill, grill the tofu for 5 minutes on both sides and set aside.
Arrange the pasta on the plates, divide the vegetables all around and place the tofu over the noodles. Douse with the marinade.

9.29 Grilled tomatoes with cheese filling

Promotes digestion, helps to digest fat, supports urination, reduces blood pressure, stimulates digestion.
Cooking time approx. 30 min
Calories p. portion: 470
2 portions
Allergens: ACG

Quantity of ingredients:
Tomato 8 pieces / 200g. (yes)
Feta cheese 0,2 lbs / 75g. (yes)
Fresh cheese 0,2 lbs / 75g. (yes)
Chicken egg 1 piece / 60g. (yes)
Olive oil 1 table spoon / 12g. (recommended)
Basil (fresh) 1 table spoon / 6g. (yes)
Salt 1 pinch / 1g. (yes)
Pepper (ground) 1 pinch / 0,5g. (yes)
Olives 1 oz / 30g. (recommended)
Rucola 1/4 lbs / 100g. (yes)
White bread (wheat bread) 4 slices / 80g. (yes)

Cooking instructions:
Hollow out tomatoes generously. Put in a casserole dish.
Mix cheese, olive oil, egg, chopped basil and flour. Season with salt and pepper and fill in the tomatoes.
Bake in the preheated oven at 210 degrees on the middle rail for 15 minutes, then switch on the oven grill and grill for a further 3 minutes (without circulating air).
Stone the olives and chop and sprinkle on the tomatoes.
Garnish tomatoes with rocket and serve with white bread.

9.30 Halibut with tomato and garlic sauce

Promotes digestion, helps to digest fat, supports urination, reduces blood pressure, good to fight rheumatism, flatulence, bladder weakness, anemia, high blood pressure, depressions, diabetes, diarrhea. Valuable omega-3 fatty acids.
Cooking time approx. 45 min
Calories p. portion: 319
5 portions
Allergens: D

Quantity of ingredients:
Rice variety any 1 cup / 120g. (yes)
Water 6 cups / 240g. (yes)
Salt 1 pinch / 1g. (yes)
Halibut (Flatfish) 2,2 lbs / 800g. (yes)
Salt 1 pinch / 1g. (yes)
Pepper (ground) 1 pinch / 0,5g. (yes)
Lemon juice 1 dash / 2g. (yes)
Bay leaf 2 pieces / 2g. (yes)
Lemon 1 piece / 30g. (yes)
Garlic 8 pieces / 10g. (yes)
Thyme dried 1 table spoon / 5g. (yes)
Olives 0,2 lbs / 75g. (recommended)
Tomato 4 pieces / 200g. (yes)
Salt 1 pinch / 1g. (yes)
Pepper (ground) 1 pinch / 0,5g. (yes)

Cooking instructions:
Cook rice with salted water (1:3).
Rinse the fish under running cold water, dab with kitchen paper and rub with salt, pepper and lemon juice.
Place the fish fillets in a casserole dish with pieces of bay leaf.

Wash the lemon hot and cut into slices, peel and halve the garlic.
Sprinkle the olives and the thyme over them.
Brew the tomatoes with hot water, skin and chop.

Mix all ingredients, season with salt and pepper and distribute around the fish.

Cook everything at 200°C/392°F for about 20 minutes.
Serve with the rice.

9.31 Hearty winter breakfast

Strengthens immune system, calms nerves and stomach, promotes digestion, detoxifying, strengthens bodily production, promotes perspiration, reduces blood lipids, stimulates, dissolves stagnation.
Cooking time approx. 20 min
Calories p. portion: 678
1 portions
Allergens: ACEG

Quantity of ingredients:
Oat meal 1 cup / 120g. (yes)
Ginger fresh 1/2 teaspoon / 1g. (yes)
Salt 1 pinch / 1g. (yes)
Onion (spring onion) 2 pieces / 40g. (yes)
Chicken egg 1 piece / 55g. (yes)
Butter organic 1 table spoon / 15g. (recommended)
Soy sauce 1 dash / 3g. (yes)

Cooking instructions:
Soak oatmeal overnight. Boil in the morning with a little ginger, salt and a spring onion or leek and then let it swell until the porridge is soft. Before serving, add a whole egg to the porridge, add the butter and season to taste with a little soy sauce.

Recommendation: Especially suitable for the cold season.

9.32 Kidney bean pot with lamb and sage

Relieves weakness, strengthens lung, spleen and stomach. Diuretic. Strengthens gastrointestinal function, expands blood vessels, prevents cancer, prevents diseases (in the elderly).
Cooking time approx. 1 1/2 hours
Calories p. portion: 391
4 portions
Allergens: F

Quantity of ingredients:
Soybean oil 2 table spoons / 30g. (recommended)
Onion white 2 pieces / 120g. (yes)
Lamb meat 5/8 oz / 200g. (yes)
Salt 1 pinch / 0,5g. (yes)
Sage 4-5 leaves / 2g. (yes)
Rosemary 1/2 teaspoon / 2g. (yes)
Thyme 1/2 teaspoon / 2g. (yes)
Kidney beans (red) 5/8 lbs - 8oz / 250g. (yes)
Water 3 cups / 750g. (yes)

Cooking instructions:
Soak kidney beans in water overnight and strain.
In a saucepan with oil, roast the onion. Dice the lamb and place in the pot.
Season with salt, sage, rosemary and thyme.
Roast lamb well and cover pot. Cook over low heat and add ten-quarters of a gallon (750ml.) of cold water after 10 minutes.
Salt again.
Heat till it boils. Add beans to it.
Simmer for at least 1 hour until the beans and meat are tender.

9.33 Lasagne with tofu cream

Harmonizes spleen and stomach, reduces Flatulence, protects the digestive system. Good to fight lack of appetite, flatulence, inflammatory bowel disease, stomach ulcers, rheumatism, heartburn, twelffinger intestinal ulcers.
Cooking time approx. 45 min
Calories p. portion: 301
4 portions
Allergens: ACEG

Quantity of ingredients:
Soy Tofu 7/8 lbs / 400g. (yes)
Chicken egg 2 pieces / 100g. (yes)
Onion white 2 pieces / 120g. (yes)
Tomato 1/4 lbs - 4oz / 100g. (yes)
Oregano dried 1 pinch / 1g. (yes)
Marjoram 1 pinch / 1g. (yes)
Peppers powder 1 pinch / 1g. (yes)
Salt 1 pinch / 1g. (yes)
Noodles (wheat, lasagne) with egg 3/8 lbs - 6oz / 150g. (yes)
Edam cheese 1/8 lbs - 2oz / 50g. (yes)

Cooking instructions:
Tofu cream: Mix tofu with eggs, onions, small tomatoes, oregano, marjoram, peppers and some sea salt put into a smooth mass using a kitchen machine with a knife or a blender.

Lasagne: Place 1/5 of the tofu cream in a casserole dish (25x15cm), cover with 3 lasagna leaves, repeat this process twice, and then finish the last fifth of the tofu cream over the pastry plates. Sprinkle with a little grated Edam and bake in the oven at 175°C/347°F for about 1/2 hour.

9.34 Lettuce with fresh cheese

The bitter substances have diuretic effect and promote the blood circulation in the digestive area. Mustard improves thyroid function, relieves rheumatism symptoms.
Cooking time approx. 5 min
Calories p. portion: 802
1 portions
Allergens: AFM

Quantity of ingredients:
Leaf salads (bitter) 2 portions / 60g. (yes)
Fresh cheese from soya 3/8 lbs - 6oz / 150g. (yes)
Mustard 1 knife tip / 1g. (yes)
Lemon juice 1 dash / 3g. (yes)
Salt 1 pinch / 1g. (yes)
Pepper (ground) 1 pinch / 0,5g. (yes)
Herbs various 2 teaspoons / 4g. (yes)
Black caraway 1 pinch / 1g. (yes)
Whole grain bread 2 slices / 40g. (yes)

Cooking instructions:
Wash lettuce and finely pluck.
Mix 150 ml cream cheese, splashes of mustard, splashes of lemon juice, 1 clove of garlic, chopped fresh herbs, pinch of pepper and crushed black cumin and pour over. Serve with wholemeal bread.

9.35 Millet with egg and butter

Calms nerves and stomach, soothes embryo during pregnancy.
Diuretic, building up, eye-enhancing, detoxifying, nerve-strengthening.
Stimulates liver function, detoxifying.
Cooking time approx. 25 min
Calories p. portion: 338
2 portions
Allergens: CG

Quantity of ingredients:
Millet 1 cup / 100g. (yes)
Ginger fresh 1/2 teaspoon / 1g. (yes)
Salt 1 pinch / 0,5g. (yes)
Parsley 2 table spoons / 16g. (yes)
Pepper powder (hot) 1 pinch / 1g. (yes)
Chicken egg 2 pieces / 100g. (yes)
Butter organic 2 table spoons / 20g. (recommended)
Nutmeg 1 pinch / 0,2g. (yes)
Water 1 1/2 cups / 200g. (yes)

Cooking instructions:
Simmer the millet with the ginger and nutmeg in the water for 5 min. and let it swell for another 30 min.
Cook and peel 1 soft egg per person; pile up the millet on plates and place 1 egg each in a hollow in the millet mountain; Put butter flakes over it. Sprinkle with chopped parsley and the rose paprika.

9.36 Mung bean stew

Relieves excessive thirst, supports urination, reduces blood lipids, relieves allergies. Strengthens spleen and stomach, strengthens the muscles. Lowers cholesterol, antiparasitic. Stimulates liver function, detoxifying.
Cooking time approx. 2 hours
Calories p. portion: 665
2 portions
Allergens:

Quantity of ingredients:
Mung bean 5/8 lbs - 8oz - 500g / 300g. (yes)
Sunflower oil 2 table spoons / 30g. (recommended)
Amaranth 1/2 teaspoon / 2g. (yes)
Fennel seeds ground 1/2 teaspoon / 2g. (yes)
Cumin (Caraway seed) 1/2 teaspoon / 2g. (yes)
Coriander 1/2 teaspoon / 2g. (yes)
Rice round grain 1/2 cup / 60g. (yes)
Water 3 cups / 300g. (yes)
Ginger fresh 1 inch / 3g. (yes)
Kombu seaweed (Saccharina japonica) 1 inch / 2g. (yes)
Salt 1 pinch / 0,5g. (yes)
Parsley 1 table spoon / 3g. (yes)

Cooking instructions:
Soak mung beans overnight.
Heat sunflower oil in a hot pot. Stir in the amaranth, fennel seeds, cumin and coriander and fry briefly; ad basmati rice, some ginger and mung beans and roast briefly.
Pour water and heat till it boils.
Add a piece of kombu alga and salt.
Simmer for 1-1/2 hours.
Garnish with parsley or coriander.

9.37 Noodle casserole with plugs and peaches

Relieves fatigue, relaxes, good to fight belching, acute or chronic obstruction of the bowel, flatulence, heartburn. Calms nerves and stomach, strengthens the defense, good to fight fungi infections.
Cooking time approx. 1 hour
Calories p. portion: 442
4 portions
Allergens: ACGO

Quantity of ingredients:
Peaches 1,1 lbs / 500g. (yes)
Noodles (wheat, ribbon noodles) with egg 5/8 oz / 200g. (yes)
Chicken egg 2 pieces / 120g. (yes)
Sugar - icing sugar 1/8 lbs - 2oz / 40g. (recommended)
Vanilla sugar natural 3 package / 3g. (yes)
Lemon peel 1/2 piece / 2g. (yes)
Cinnamon ground 1/4 teaspoon / 1g. (yes)
Curd cheese 20% 5/8 lbs - 8oz / 250g. (yes)
Butter organic 2 teaspoons / 8g. (recommended)
Strawberry jam 4 table spoons / 50g. (yes)

Cooking instructions:
Preheat oven to 180°C/356°F.
Put Peaches briefly in boiling water, drain and peel off the skin. Cut peaches into small slices.
Cook noodles in plenty of salted water until firm, drain, chill off cold and drain.
Separate eggs. Stir egg yolks with icing sugar, vanilla sugar, grated lemon zest and cinnamon until fluffy with the whisk. Stir in the curd

cheese. Add the noodles.
Beat the egg whites into firm snow and carefully lift them under the pasta.
Spread a baking dish thinly with butter. Alternating pate noodle mixture and peach slices into the form layers. Finish with the pasta mixture. Sprinkle the casserole with butter flakes and bake in a preheated oven for 3o minutes. Serve portion by portion with a tablespoon of jam.

9.38 Noodles with turkeymeat and pineapple

Solves bile-, kidney- and bladder stones, provides Vitamin C, strengthens blood, strengthens bone marrow, reduces inflammation, supports urination.
Cooking time approx. 45 min
Calories p. portion: 292
4 portions
Allergens: ACGL

Quantity of ingredients:
Noodles (whole grain) with egg 5/8 oz / 200g. (yes)
Pineapple 5/8 oz / 200g. (yes)
Water 1/2 cup / 50g. (yes)
Turkey breast meat 5/8 oz / 200g. (yes)
Rapeseed oil 1 table spoon / 12g. (recommended)
Garlic 1 piece / 2g. (yes)
Basic recipe for a vegetable soup (nutritious) 1/2 cup / 100g. (yes)
Cow's milk (whole milk 3.5% fat) 2/3 cup / 180g. (recommended)
Fresh cheese 0,2 lbs / 75g. (yes)
Curry 3 teaspoons / 6g. (yes)
Salt 1 pinch / 1g. (yes)
Pepper (ground) 1 pinch / 0,5g. (yes)
Pomegranate 1 piece / 300g. (yes)
Coconut flakes 1 table spoon / 6g. (yes)

Cooking instructions:
Cook the noodles in salt water. Cut the pineapple into cubes and leave for 5 min. to simmer in water. Cut the meat sliced in strips and roast them in the oil. Add the chopped garlic and the pineapple sliced. Add about 50 ml of the ananas juice and stir in the vegetable broth. Add the milk and the fresh cheese, then stir well until the fresh cheese is completely dissolved. Now add the curry and simmer for a few minutes until a creamy consistency is reached. Season with salt and pepper. Now add the noodles in the finished sauce. Cut the pomegranate and

release the seeds. Distribute as many kernels on the dressed noodles. Whoever likes it can spread coconut chips over it.

9.39 Pancakes with spinach and parmesan

Promotes bowel movement, improves blood circulation, forcing spleen and bowel, strengthens immune system, good to fight loss of appetite, flatulence, high blood pressure, depressions, diabetes, constipation.
Cooking time approx. 25 min
Calories p. portion: 330
6 portions
Allergens: ACGL

Quantity of ingredients:
Wholemeal flour 1/4 lbs - 4oz / 100g. (yes)
Wheat flour 1/4 lbs - 4oz / 100g. (yes)
Chicken egg 4 pieces / 200g. (yes)
Cow's milk (whole milk 3.5% fat) 1 1/2 cups / 400g. (recommended)
Salt 1 pinch / 1g. (yes)
Sunflower oil 1 table spoon / 15g. (recommended)
Olive oil 1 table spoon / 15g. (recommended)
Onion white 1 piece / 50g. (yes)
Parsley 1/2 bunch / 80g. (yes)
Basic recipe for a vegetable soup (nutritious) 1/2 cup / 150g. (yes)
Basil (fresh) 1/4 teaspoon / 1g. (yes)
Nutmeg 1 pinch / 0,3g. (yes)
Créme fraiche cheese 2 table spoons / 45g. (recommended)
Spinach 1,3 lbs / 600g. (yes)
Salt 1 pinch / 1g. (yes)
Pepper (ground) 1 pinch / 0,1g. (yes)
Parmesan 1/8 lbs - 2oz / 60g. (recommended)

Cooking instructions:
Stir flour, eggs and milk and a pinch of salt with the whisk until smooth. From the dough, fry pancakes crispy brown on both sides.
Heat oil in a small saucepan. Fry the finely chopped onion until tender. Stir in chopped parsley, sauté briefly. Add the vegetable broth according to the basic recipe, season with basil and nutmeg. Cover and simmer for 15 minutes, add crème fraiche and finely puree.
Cook the washed, drizzled spinach with a little salt in a closed pan over a moderate heat in 3 minutes, drain in a sieve and cut into small pieces. Add the spinach to the sauce, heat briefly. Add parmesan in the mix.
Fill the pancakes with the cream spinach.

9.40 Paprika turkey with rice and lettuce

Strengthens blood and bone marrow.
Cooking time approx. 1 hour
Calories p. portion: 391
6 portions
Allergens: AG

Quantity of ingredients:
Olive oil 2 table spoons / 20g. (recommended)
Onion white 1 piece / 60g. (yes)
Peppers (rose peppers) 2 table spoons / 14g. (yes)
Chicken meat 1 piece / 800g. (yes)
Water 1 cup / 250g. (yes)
Salt 1 pinch / 1g. (yes)
Spelled wholemeal flour 1 table spoon / 7g. (yes)
Sour cream 15% fat 5/8 lbs - 8oz / 250g. (yes)
Water 6 cups / 400g. (yes)
Rice Basmati 1 cup / 120g. (yes)
Salt 1 pinch / 1g. (yes)
Lettuce 1 piece / 200g. (yes)
Olive oil 2 table spoons / 20g. (recommended)
Lemon juice 1/2 piece / 15g. (yes)
Herbs various 2 table spoons / 6g. (yes)

Cooking instructions:
Heat the oil in a saucepan and fry the onions in a golden yellow.
Sprinkle plenty of peppers over the onion and stir well so that it does not burn. Put the pot aside.
In a casserole, fry the chicken parts from one side; turn the meat over, spread the onion above and fry the chicken parts from the other side.
As soon as they have taken on a deep red color, pour the vegetable broth and heat till it boils.
Season with salt, reduce the heat and stew the chicken for 45 minutes or until cooked.
Put the poultry parts together with cooking liquid in a bowl and set aside.
Add 2 to 3 tbsp of flour to the casserole and gradually add the cooking solution again, stirring constantly until the sauce is thickened.
Stir in the sour cream or yoghurt, put the poultry pieces back into the pot and heat again well, but do not boil.
Place the rice with the salted water, bring to the boil and simmer until the rice is tender.

Wash and dry the lettuce. Pluck small and put in a bowl.
In a cup, mix the olive oil, the lemon juice, the salt and fresh chopped herbs and pour over the salad.

9.41 Pea dish

Supports urination, calms nerves and stomach, soothes embryo during pregnancy. Strengthens gastrointestinal function, prevents diseases.
Cooking time approx. 1-2 hours
Calories p. portion: 406
1 portions
Allergens: CE

Quantity of ingredients:
Peas 3/8 lbs - 6oz (dried) / 150g. (yes)
Lemon 1 piece / 40g. (yes)
Juniper berry 6 pieces / 2g. (yes)
Sunflower oil 1 teaspoon / 3g. (recommended)
Pepper white (ground) 1 pinch / 0,3g. (yes)
Bay leaf 3 leaves / 2g. (yes)
Onion white 1 piece / 50g. (yes)
Thyme 1 teaspoon / 2g. (yes)
Ginger fresh 1/2 teaspoon / 1g. (yes)
Chicken egg 1 piece / 60g. (yes)
Wakame 1 inch / 2g. (yes)
Salt 1 pinch / 1g. (yes)
Soy sauce per taste / 2g. (yes)

Cooking instructions:
Soak dried peas in plenty of cold water for several hours or overnight.
Pour away soaking water and wash peas thoroughly.

Place the peas with about 1 1/2 l of cold water and heat till it boils; cook without lid for 5 minutes; scoop up the foam that forms; only then add the following ingredients: a slice of lemon, juniper berries, oil, peppercorns, bay leaves, chopped onion, dried thyme, chopped ginger, simmer about 2 strips of wakame or 1 tbsp Hijiki with lid closed for 1 - 2 hours; After 1 hour, try if the peas are already soft, because the cooking time changes with the soaking time and the age of aging; when the peas are cooked, remove the lemon slice, juniper berries and peppercorns; with salt, soy sauce, lemon juice to taste.
Note: The dish can be refrigerated for 3-4 days and heated in portions.
Serve with: crispy vegetables, rice or millet steamed in water.

9.42 Polenta with fried egg

Calms nerves, forcing spleen and stomach, lets urine and bile juice flow, prevents cancer, forcing spleen, improves blood circulation, encourages growth, dissolves stagnation.
Cooking time approx. 15 min
Calories p. portion: 410
2 portions
Allergens: CG

Quantity of ingredients:
Water 1 1/2 cups / 200g. (yes)
Corn Grease (Polenta) 1 cup / 120g. (yes)
Ginger fresh 1 pinch / 0,5g. (yes)
Butter organic 1/2 teaspoon / 2g. (recommended)
Pepper (ground) 1 pinch / 0,2g. (yes)
Nutmeg 1 pinch / 0,2g. (yes)
Salt 1 pinch / 0,5g. (yes)
Lemon juice 1 dash / 1g. (yes)
Pepper powder (hot) 1 pinch / 0,3g. (yes)
Chicken egg 4 pieces / 250g. (yes)
Chives 2 table spoons / 14g. (yes)

Cooking instructions:
Stir in a saucepan with hot water polenta and a little ginger; swell until the polenta is cooked.
Add a piece of butter, pepper, nutmeg, salt, a few drops of lemon, a pinch of rose paprika.
Put the polenta in a fireproof bowl.
Put 1 fried egg per person on top; bake in the oven for a few minutes, so that the egg yolk is still liquid.
Sprinkle with ground pepper, finely chopped chives and a little salt.

9.43 Potatoes with wild garlic-curd cheese

Improves digestion, regenerates skin, supports urination, lowers cholesterol. Helps to fight stomach pressure, belching, diabetes, acute or chronic constipation of the intestine. Improves the flow characteristics of the blood.
Cooking time approx. 20 min
Calories p. portion: 254
2 portions
Allergens: G

Quantity of ingredients:
Potato 3/4 lbs / 300g. (yes)
Salt 1 pinch / 0,1g. (yes)
Wild garlic (garlic spinach) 2 handful / 30g. (yes)
Curd cheese 20% 5/8 lbs - 8oz / 250g. (yes)
Yogurt (natural, 1.5% fat) 2 table spoons / 20g. (yes)
Salt 1 pinch / 1g. (yes)

Cooking instructions:
Cook potatoes in salted water and peel.
Wash he wild garlic leaves and carefully dried and cut into fine strips.
Mix the cottage cheese, yogurt and salt and mix in the chopped wild garlic pieces. Serve with the potatoes.
In the season in which no wild garlic grows the wild garlic pesto can be used.

9.44 Pumpkin dumplings with tomato and parsley sauce

Protects the digestive system. Good to fight loss of appetite, flatulence, calms nerves and stomach, helps to digest fat, reduces blood pressure, stimulates liver function, dissolves stagnation.
Cooking time approx. 30 min
Calories p. portion: 380
2 portions
Allergens: ACG

Quantity of ingredients:
Hokkaido pumpkin 1/4 lbs - 4oz / 100g. (yes)
Chicken egg 2 pieces / 120g. (yes)
Wheat flour 1/2-1/3 cup / 120g. (yes)
Salt 1 pinch / 1g. (yes)
Pepper (ground) 1 pinch / 0,5g. (yes)
Nutmeg 1 pinch / 0,2g. (yes)
Lemon peel 1/2 teaspoon / 2g. (yes)
Parmesan 2 table spoons / 20g. (recommended)
Onion (spring onion) 2 pieces / 40g. (yes)
Tomato 1/4 lbs - 4oz / 100g. (yes)
Parsley 1/2 bunch / 50g. (yes)
Salt 1 pinch / 1g. (yes)

Cooking instructions:
Peel the pumpkin with a sharp knife, remove the seeds and cut the pulp into large cubes. Wrap pumpkin in aluminum foil, bake in preheated oven at 200°C/392°F for 20 minutes. Pour off any spilled pumpkin juice. Finely crush the pumpkin with the fork. Stir pumpkin and egg until smooth. Stir in so much flour until a dough is formed, from which dumplings can be cut off. Season the mixture with lemon zest, salt, pepper and nutmeg.
Cut off small dumplings with a teaspoon. Leave pumpkin dumplings in boiling salted water for approx. 7 minutes.

Roast the onion in a frying pan until lightly fry the tomato cubes, salt and the chopped parsley.

Arrange pumpkin dumplings in portions with the tomato parsley sauce. Parmesan to hand.

9.45 Rhubarb cake with sprinkles

Laxative, antipyretic. Protects the digestive system. Detoxifying, affects anorexia, good to fight flatulence, inflammatory bowel disease, brittle nails and hair. Relieves pain, detoxifying, against dry skin, acne, eczema.
Cooking time approx. 1 1/2 hours
Calories p. portion: 476
8 portions
Allergens: AG

Quantity of ingredients:
Wheat flour 7/8 lbs / 400g. (yes)
Cow's milk (whole milk 3.5% fat) 1 cup / 200g. (recommended)
Yeast 1 oz / 30g. (yes)
Honey 2 teaspoons / 5g. (yes)
Sunflower oil 2 teaspoons / 5g. (recommended)
Lemon peel 1 piece / 3g. (yes)
Salt 1 pinch / 1g. (yes)
Rhubarb 2,2 lbs / 800g. (yes)
Margarine 1/4 lbs - 4oz / 120g. (recommended)
Wheat flour 3/4 lbs / 300g. (yes)
Vanilla sugar natural 2 pinches / 1g. (yes)
Cinnamon ground 2 pinches / 1g. (yes)
Honey 5 table spoons / 50g. (yes)

Cooking instructions:
Mix flour, grated lemon peel and salt.
Heat milk gently and mix with yeast and honey.
Then add the flour mixture and the oil and knead vigorously. Cover the dough and let it rise in a warm place until it reaches twice the amount. (about 30 minutes)

For the sprinkles, mix flour with vanilla and cinnamon, then add honey and margarine and crumble to a crumbly mass. Keep the sprinkles dough cool.

Lay out a baking sheet with parchment paper.
Knead the dough for the bottom again, roll it out, place it on the baking sheet and let it rise for another 10 minutes.

Clean the rhubarb, wash it, halve lengthwise and cut into pieces of approx. 3 cm. Spread the pieces on the rolled out dough and crumble the sprinkles over the cake.

Place the cake in the preheated oven at 175 ° C and bake for about 40 minutes.

9.46 Ribbon noodles with leaf spinach

Promotes digestion, improves blood circulation, forcing spleen and intestine, improves pancreatic function, Good to fight loss of appetite, flatulence, inflammatory bowel disease, obesity, stomach ulcers, stomach cramps, rheumatism, heartburn, twelffinger intestinal ulcers.
Cooking time approx. 45 min
Calories p. portion: 722
2 portions
Allergens: ACG

Quantity of ingredients:
Spinach 5/8 lbs - 8oz / 250g. (yes)
Salt 1 pinch / 1g. (yes)
Noodles (wheat, ribbon noodles) with egg 5/8 oz / 200g. (yes)
Olive oil 1 table spoon / 15g. (recommended)
Onion (spring onion) 1 piece / 20g. (yes)
Cream, sweet 30% 1/2 cup / 100g. (recommended)
Créme fraiche cheese 1/2 teaspoon / 6g. (recommended)
Thyme dried 1/2 teaspoon / 2g. (yes)
Basil (fresh) 1/2 teaspoon / 2g. (yes)

Oregano dried 1/2 teaspoon / 2g. (yes)
Nutmeg 1 pinch / 0,5g. (yes)
Pepper (ground) 1 pinch / 0,5g. (yes)
Parmesan 1/2 oz / 20g. (recommended)
Pine nuts 1 table spoon / 15g. (recommended)
Black caraway 1 pinch / 1g. (yes)

Cooking instructions:
Put the dripping wet spinach together with a little salt for 3 minutes ina pot, then drain in a sieve. Then finely cut.

Boil tagliatelle in plenty of salted water.

Heat the oil in a skillet and fry the spring onions rings. Add cream, crème fraîche, thyme, basil, oregano and nutmeg. Stir in the sauce while stirring. Add the spinach, heat briefly, season with nutmeg, salt and pepper.
Drain pasta and mix with the spinach. Season with salt and pepper. Portion noodles and serve with parmesan and pine nuts. Sprinkle the black cumin over it.

9.47 Scrambled eggs with rocket and herbs

Calms nerves and stomach, promotes digestion, detoxifying, strengthens bodily fluids production, promotes perspiration, reduces blood lipids, stimulates, dissolves stagnation, stimulates liver function, harmonizes liver and spleen, strengthens eyesight, detoxifying.
Cooking time approx. 10 min
Calories p. portion: 360
1 portions
Allergens: CG

Quantity of ingredients:
Butter organic 2 table spoons / 20g. (recommended)
Ginger fresh 1 knife tip / 1g. (yes)
Chicken egg 2 pieces / 120g. (yes)
Pepper (ground) 1 pinch / 0,5g. (yes)
Coriander 1 pinch / 1g. (yes)
Parsley 2 table spoons / 16g. (yes)
Rucola 2 handful / 30g. (yes)
Oregano dried 1 teaspoon / 2g. (yes)
Savory 1 pinch / 0,5g. (yes)

Cooking instructions:
Melt a piece of butter in a hot pan; add fine cutted ginger and roast it shortly. Mix in 1 egg whipped, pepper freshly ground, a pinch of coriander, bean cabbage, some salt, parsley chopped, rocket and oregano cut into small pieces until the egg stalls, but still juicy. Garnish: millet, polenta, potatoes, toasted bread. The dish is wholesome, without carbohydrate.

9.48 Semolina dumpling soup

Reduces blood pressure, strengthens immune system, prevents cancer, reduces radiation damage, dissolves stagnation, promotes weight loss. Good to fight immunodeficiency, loss of appetite, flatulence, high blood pressure, depressions, diabetes, diarrhea.
Cooking time approx. 1 hour
Calories p. portion: 287
3 portions
Allergens: ACGLO

Quantity of ingredients:
Butter organic 1/8 lbs - 2oz / 40g. (recommended)
Chicken egg 1 piece / 65g. (yes)
Salt 1 pinch / 1g. (yes)
Pepper (ground) 1 pinch / 0,5g. (yes)
Nutmeg 1 pinch / 1g. (yes)
Wheat semolina 3 oz / 80g. (yes)
Basic recipe for a beef soup (warming) 2 cup / 500g. (yes)
Parsley 1 table spoon / 10g. (yes)
Chives 1 table spoon / 10g. (yes)

Cooking instructions:
Knead the ingredients for the dumplings to a firm dough and allow to swell for 30 minutes. Heat the broth (basic recipe for a beef broth warming). Then cut out with a spoon dumplings, place in the prepared broth and let stand for 20 minutes. Before serving, chop parsley and sprinkle with thinly sliced chives.

9.49 Sliced chicken with walnuts and sherry

Strengthens blood, strengthens bone marrow, strengthens gastrointestinal function, expands blood vessels, prevents cancer, promotes perspiration, reduces blood lipids, stimulates.
Cooking time approx. 25 min
Calories p. portion: 304
4 portions
Allergens: EGHN

Quantity of ingredients:
Butter organic 2 table spoons / 35g. (recommended)
Walnuts 2 table spoons / 25g. (recommended)
Ginger fresh 1/2 teaspoon / 2g. (yes)
Onion (shallot) 2 pieces / 40g. (yes)
Salt 1 pinch / 1g. (yes)
Chicken meat 3/4 lbs / 300g. (yes)
Peppers powder 1 pinch / 1g. (yes)
Sesame, white 1 teaspoon / 2g. (recommended)
Black fungus mushroom 4 pieces / 3g. (yes)
Shiitake, dried 4 pieces / 5g. (yes)
Soy sauce 1 dash / 3g. (yes)
Rice (whole grain) 1 cup / 120g. (yes)
Water 6 cups / 550g. (yes)
Salt 1 pinch / 1g. (yes)

Cooking instructions:
Heat butter or sesame oil in a hot pan; Sauté walnuts, copious grated ginger, chopped shallots or onions; Add the salt and the sliced chicken and sauté everything; Rose paprika, roasted sesame, soaked black fungus, shiitake mushrooms or mushrooms; with a shot sherry; infuse with water; Simmer for 5 to 10 minutes until the meat is cooked; Season with soy sauce.

Place the rice in salted water, heat till it boils and let it simmer over low heat for about 15 minutes.

This fits: lamb's lettuce, Radicchio

9.50 Spicy cake with dates

Good to fight loss of appetite, flatulence, inflammatory bowel disease, obesity, gout, stomach ulcers, stomach cramps, rheumatism, heartburn. Calms nerves and stomach, improves blood circulation.
Cooking time approx. 1 1/2 hours
Calories p. portion: 808
4 portions
Allergens: ACGO

Quantity of ingredients:
Sunflower oil 1/2 cup / 100g. (recommended)
Sugar white 5/8 oz / 200g. (recommended)
Cow's milk (whole milk 3.5% fat) 1/2 cup / 100g. (recommended)
Wheat flour 5/8 lbs - 8oz / 250g. (yes)
Cocoa 1/8 lbs - 2oz / 40g. (yes)
Dates dried 1/8 lbs - 2oz / 50g. (yes)
Chicken egg 3 pieces / 180g. (yes)
Clove 1/2 teaspoon / 1g. (yes)
Cinnamon ground 1 1/2 tea spoon / 3g. (yes)
Nutmeg 1 pinch / 0,5g. (yes)
Baking powder 1/2 package / 1,5g. (yes)
Butter organic 1 teaspoon / 2g. (recommended)
Wheat flour 1 teaspoon / 2g. (yes)

Cooking instructions:
Separate eggs. Stir egg whites until stiff and set aside.
Add oil, sugar, egg yolk to a bowl and stir until frothy.
Add the flour, cocoa and baking powder, stir. Stir in the milk. Now add the minced dates and the spices (the cloves as grated powder) to the mixture and mix with low speed of the hand mixer.
Now, take the stiffly egg white spoonful carefully under.
Put the dough in a greased, floured mold and bake at 200°C/392°F for 70 minutes.

9.51 Sweet potato pancakes with basil pesto

Strengthens the immune system, reduces fat, Improves digestion, calms nerves and stomach, dissolves stones, improves blood circulation, strengthens the muscles, antioxidativ.
Cooking time approx. 30 min
Calories p. portion: 625
3 portions
Allergens: ACH

Quantity of ingredients:
Sweet potato 4 pieces / 500g. (yes)
Onion read 1/2 piece / 30g. (yes)
Basil 1 table spoon / 10g. (yes)
Chicken egg 2 pieces / 140g. (yes)
Spelled wholemeal flour 3 oz / 80g. (yes)
Salt 1 pinch / 0,5g. (yes)
Olive oil 1/4 cup / 20g. (recommended)
Salt 1 teaspoon (coarse) / 3g. (yes)
Basil Handful / 15g. (yes)
Parsley Handful / 15g. (yes)
Garlic 2 cloves / 3g. (yes)
Walnuts 1/8 lbs - 2oz / 60g. (recommended)
Olive oil 2 table spoons / 20g. (recommended)

Cooking instructions:
Sweet Potato Buffer: Wash the sweet potato thoroughly, but do not peel, and grate into a large bowl. Add onion, basil, egg and flour, mix well and sprinkle with salt. The mixture can be formed into buffers. Bake in a preheated tube on a baking tray coated with oil for 4 to 5 minutes on both sides.

Basil Pesto: Add the salt, chopped basil and parsley and crushed garlic in a small bowl and crush (if available, use the mortar). Add the grated walnuts. While stirring, add enough olive oil until the desired consistency is achieved.

9.52 Tofu-Black Bean Chili with Rice

Supports urination, lowers cholesterol, prevents arteriosclerosis, for the drainage of the body overweight and high blood pressure, strengthens immune system.
Cooking time approx. 45 min
Calories p. portion: 344
4 portions
Allergens: AEL

Quantity of ingredients:
Rapeseed oil 1/4 cup / 60g. (recommended)
Onion white 2 pieces / 120g. (yes)
Peppers 1 piece / 20g. (yes)
Pepper Cayenne 1 pinch / 0,5g. (yes)

Coriander 1 teaspoon / 2g. (yes)
Thyme 1 teaspoon / 2g. (yes)
Clove 1 teaspoon / 2g. (yes)
Spelled wholemeal flour 2 table spoons / 16g. (yes)
Sherry (whine) 1 table spoon / 8g. (yes)
Soy Tofu 5/8 lbs - 8oz / 250g. (yes)
Black beans 2 cans (400g) / 400g. (yes)
Basic recipe for a chicken soup (warming) 1 1/2 cups / 300g. (yes)
Bay leaf 1 piece / 0,2g. (yes)
Garlic 6 pieces / 8g. (yes)
Water 6 cups / 400g. (yes)
Rice Basmati 1 cup / 120g. (yes)

Cooking instructions:
Heat the oil at medium temperature in a large saucepan, add onions, paprika and chili powder and fry for 2 minutes until the onions are glassy.
Add the remaining spices, stirring constantly, stirring until the aroma rises.
Dust the flour, fry for 2 minutes and make sure that the paste-like spice mixture does not burn.
Deglaze with sherry, add the black beans (tin) and mix with the spices.
Add the chicken broth, add the bay leaf and stir in the chopped garlic.
Simmer the beans for 30 minutes and add some chicken stock if needed.
Cook the tofu cubes during the last 10 minutes. The tofu can easily disintegrate and should therefore be lifted very gently with a wooden spoon.
Finally, pick out the bay leaf and serve the tofu black bean chili with rice.

9.53 Tomato with mozzarella

Promotes digestion, helps to digest fat, supports urination, reduces blood pressure. Affects anorexia, good to fight flatulence, inflammatory bowel disease, bloating and nausea. Relaxing and reassuring.
Cooking time approx. 5 min
Calories p. portion: 436
1 portions
Allergens: AG

Quantity of ingredients:
Mozzarella 1 piece / 50g. (yes)
Tomato 2 pieces / 100g. (yes)
Salt 1 pinch / 1g. (yes)
Basil (fresh) 5 leaves / 6g. (yes)
Olive oil 2 table spoons / 20g. (recommended)
White bread (wheat bread) 2 slices / 40g. (yes)

Cooking instructions:
Cut tomatoes and mozzarella into slices. Serve with salt, basil and olive oil. Serve with white bread.

9.54 Turkey breast with vegetables (Asian)

Strengthens blood, strengthens bone marrow, dissolves stagnation, promotes digestion and is goo to fight high blood pressure. Rice to drain the body at overweight and high blood pressure.
Cooking time approx. 45 min
Calories p. portion: 535
2 portions
Allergens: AEN

Quantity of ingredients:
Rice variety any 1 cup / 120g. (yes)
Water 6 cups / 240g. (yes)
Turkey breast meat 5/8 oz / 200g. (yes)
Ginger fresh 1/3 inch / 3g. (yes)
Garlic 1 piece / 2g. (yes)
Soy sauce 2 table spoons / 20g. (yes)
Wheat flour 2 teaspoons / 15g. (yes)
Onion (spring onion) 2 pieces / 40g. (yes)
Peppers 1/2 piece / 10g. (yes)
Champignon 8 pieces / 30g. (yes)
Sesame oil 2 table spoons / 20g. (recommended)
Soy sauce 1 table spoon / 12g. (yes)
Curry 1 pinch / 2g. (yes)
Turmeric (yellow root) 1 pinch / 2g. (yes)
Cashews 2 teaspoons / 25g. (recommended)

Cooking instructions:
Cook the rice in salted water.
Cut the turkey meat into thin strips. Peel and dice the ginger and garlic. Put together with the meat strips in a bowl. Mix 1 tbsp of soy sauce with

the wheat starch and stir until smooth. Add to the meat and marinate for 30 minutes. Wash spring onions and peppers, clean and cut into small pieces. Clean and quarter the mushrooms.
Put one tablespoon of sesame oil in a pan and sauté and warm the marinated turkey. Now add the remaining oil to the pan and fry the other vegetables in it. Now add the meat and season with soy sauce and spices. Serve with the rice. Sprinkle the cashews over the dish before serving.

9.55 Vanilla cream with berries

Weakness, chronic constipation of the intestine, weight loss, laxative, detoxifying, blood detoxifying. Strengthens the defense. Good to fight fungi infections.
Cooking time approx. 15 min
Calories p. portion: 278
4 portions
Allergens: G

Quantity of ingredients:
Curd cheese 20% 7/8 lbs / 400g. (yes)
Yogurt (natural, 1.5% fat) 3/8 lbs - 6oz / 150g. (yes)
Sugar brown 2 teaspoons / 8g. (recommended)
Acerola fruit nectar or powder 1 teaspoon / 2g. (yes)
Vanilla sugar natural 3 package / 3g. (yes)
Cream (30% fat) 1/4 lbs - 4oz / 125g. (recommended)
Strawberries 1/4 lbs - 4oz / 100g. (yes)
Raspberry 1/4 lbs - 4oz / 100g. (yes)
Blackberry´s 1/4 lbs - 4oz / 100g. (yes)
Blueberry 1/4 lbs - 4oz / 100g. (yes)

Cooking instructions:
Mix the curd cheese, yoghurt, sugar, acerola and vanilla sugar with a hand mixer or whisk until smooth. Beat the whipped cream very stiff, mix it under the cream. Arrange vanilla cream in portions with the berries.

9.56 Wild garlic pesto

Improves the flow characteristics of the blood, high vitamin C content, stomach- und blood detoxifying, good to fight arteriosclerosis, high blood pressure.
Cooking time approx. 10 min
Calories p. portion: 796
2 portions
Allergens: G

Quantity of ingredients:
Wild garlic (garlic spinach) 1/4 lbs - 4oz / 125g. (yes)
Parmesan 1 oz / 30g. (recommended)
Pine nuts 1/8 lbs - 2oz / 50g. (recommended)
Olive oil 1/4 lbs - 4oz / 125g. (recommended)
Salt 1 pinch / 1g. (yes)
Pepper (ground) 1 pinch / 0,3g. (yes)

Cooking instructions:
Fresh wild garlic: Wash the wild garlic leaves and dry them carefully. Cut the wild garlic leaves into fine strips. Dried wild garlic: Leave approx. 80g in 40g of water for 10 minutes.
Carefully roast the pine nuts. The pine nuts should be light brown after roasting. Cut the pine nuts very finely with a large knife or rub them with a nut mill. Pick up some of the seeds to decorate the pesto later.
Place all ingredients in a tall container and chop and mix with a blender. Put the pesto in a bowl or in a glass.
In the fridge, the pesto lasts a while (days to weeks) and is therefore a way to preserve bear's garlic.
You can eat wild garlic pesto as sauce with spaghetti, but it also tastes great with potatoes or bread.

9.57 Zucchini with basil pesto

Good to fight bloating and nausea. Relaxing and reassuring, promotes digestion, forcing spleen and digestive system, detoxifying, strengthens the muscles and bones, diuretic, supports urination, dissolves stagnation.
Cooking time approx. 25 min
Calories p. portion: 468
3 portions
Allergens: ACGHL

Quantity of ingredients:
Basil (fresh) 1 Bunch / 125g. (yes)
Olive oil 1 table spoon / 20g. (recommended)
Almond 1 table spoon / 15g. (recommended)
Parmesan 1 oz / 30g. (recommended)
Basic recipe for a vegetable soup 2 table spoons / 45g. (yes)
Lemon peel 1 teaspoon / 3g. (yes)
Lemon 1 teaspoon / 3g. (yes)
Oregano dried 2 teaspoons / 15g. (yes)
Ground 1 pinch / 1g. (yes)
Salt 1 pinch / 1g. (yes)
Pepper (ground) 1 pinch / 1g. (yes)
Noodles (wheat, spaghetti) with egg 5/8 oz / 200g. (yes)
Salt 1 pinch / 1g. (yes)
Olive oil 1 table spoon / 15g. (recommended)
Onion (spring onion) 2 pieces / 40g. (yes)
Zucchini 5/8 lbs - 8oz / 250g. (yes)

Cooking instructions:
Mix Basil, olive oil, grated almonds, parmesan, vegetable broth and grated lemon peel to a smooth cream puree. Season the pesto with salt, oregano, cumin and pepper.

Boil the spaghetti with a little salt in plenty of water.

Heat the olive oil in a pan and fry the spring onions while stirring. Add zucchini and fry briefly with stirring. The zucchini should be soft with a bite. Season the zucchini with salt.

In a bowl, mix well-drained spaghetti with zucchini and pesto. Season the spaghetti with salt and pepper.

Recommended for dysphagia, loss of appetite, potassium and magnesium requirements.

10 Effects of food

10.1 Use ingredients: recommendable

Acai powder
Almond
Almond marzipan
Aloe juice
Anchovy / Sardine
Avocado
Bitter Herb liqueur
Brazil nuts
Brie cheese
Butter organic
Camembert
Cashews
Chestnut puree
Chestnuts
Corn germ oil
Cow's milk (whole milk 3.5% fat)
Cream (30% fat)
Cream 10% coffee cream
Cream sour 30%
Cream, sweet 30%
Créme fraiche cheese
Curd cheese 40%
Duck (slaughtered)
Emmental cheese
Feta cheese
Fox nut, gorgon nut, makhana
Goose
Goose parts
Gorgonzola
Gouda cheese
Hazelnuts
Hibiscus
Kudzu
Lily bulbs
Linseed oil
Mackerel
Maple syrup
Margarine
Margarine (diet)
Mascarpone cheese

Olive oil
Olives
Olives green
Palm oil
Parmesan
Peanut (roasted)
Peanuts
Pine nuts
Pistachios
Poppy
Puff pastry
Pumpkin seed oil
Pumpkin seeds
Rapeseed oil
Salmon
Sesame oil
Sesame oil roasted
Sesame paste (Tahini)
Sesame, black
Sesame, white
Soybean oil
Sugar - icing sugar
Sugar brown
Sugar candy white
Sugar cane sugar
Sugar fructose - fruit sugar
Sugar glucose - grapes sugar
Sugar Milk Sugar
Sugar molasses
Sugar palm sugar
Sugar white
Sunflower oil
Sunflower seeds
Supplementary nutrition
Tuna
Walnut oil
Walnuts
Walnuts roasted
Wheat germ oil
Yogurt (natural, 3.5% fat)

10.2 Use ingredients: yes

Acerola fruit nectar or powder
Adzuki beans
Agar agar (kelp)
Agave nectar
Agrimony
Almond milk

Almond puree
Amaranth
Amaranth Pops
Angelica root
Anise (Common Fennel)
Apple (sour)

Apple (sweet)
Apple juice (natural cloudy)
Apple puree
Apricot
Apricot dried
Apricot jam
Apricot nectar
Apricots
Apricots juice
Arrowroot
Artichoke
Asparagus (green or white)
Aubergine
Baking powder
Balm
Bamboo shoots
Banana
Banana (cooking banana)
Banchatee (green tea)
barberry
Barley
Barley flour
Barley grass powder
Barley grouts
Barley malt
Barley not peeled
Basic recipe for a beef soup
Basic recipe for a beef soup (warming)
Basic recipe for a chicken soup
(warming)
Basic recipe for a duck soup
Basic recipe for a fish soup
Basic recipe for a rice soup (Congee)
Basic recipe for a vegetable soup
(nutritious)
Basil
Basil (fresh)
Batavia
Bay leaf
Bean oil
Beans (green, fresh)
Bearberry leaf
Beef bone marrow
Beef fillet
Beef heart
Beef heart (calf)
Beef kidney
Beef liver
Beef lungs (calf)
Beef meat
Beef meat (calf)
Beef meatbones
Beef Oxtail pieces
Beef soup meat

Beef stomach
Beer (alcohol-free)
Beer (alcohol-reduced)
Beer (Pils)
Beer (Top-fermented German dark
beer)
Berries of the season
Berry juice
Bitter Lemon
Bitter liqueur
Bitter orange peel
Black beans
Black caraway
Black fungus mushroom
Black tea
Blackberry dried (unripe fruit)
Blackberry jam
Blackberry leaves
Blackberry´s
Black-eyed peas
Blackthorn (Sloe)
Blue mallow tee
Blueberry
Blueberry dried
Blueberry jam
Blueberry juice
Bocksdorn fruits (Fructus Lycii, Goji,
goji berry dried
Boletus mushroom
Borage
Borage oil
Boxhorn clover seeds
Bread roll
Bread with carob kernel flour
Breadcrumbs (wheat bread, bread roll)
Broad beans (thick beans)
Broccoli
Brown ale
Brussels sprouts
Buckbean
Buckwheat
Buckwheat (roasted) Kasha
Buckwheat whole grain
Bulgur (cereals)
Burdock root tea
Bush beans
Butter (half fat)
Butter beans white
Buttermilk
Calamari
Campari
Cantaloupe
Capers in olive oil
Carambola (Star fruit)

Cardamom
Carob flour, St. john's bread
Carp
Carrot
Carrot (Early Carrot)
Carrot juice without sugar
Cauliflower
Caviar
Celery root
Celery sticks
Cereal coffee
Chamomile
Chamomile tea
Champignon
Channa-Dal
Chanterelle
Chard
Chenpi (chinese tangerine bowl)
Cherry
Cherry (sour)
Cherry compote
Cherry juice
Chervil
Chervil dried
Chicken Blood
Chicken egg
Chicken egg white
Chicken heart
Chicken liver
Chicken meat
Chicken stomach
Chicken yolk
Chickpeas
Chickweed
Chicory
Chili (pod or ground)
Chinese cabbage
Chinese pearl barley
Chives
Chlorella (fresh water)
Chocolate
Chocolate (Diabetic)
Chrysanthemum blossom tea
Cinnamon ground
Cinnamon sticks
Clarified butter
Clementine
Clementines
Clove
Cocoa
Coconut fat
Coconut flakes
Coconut grated
Coconut meat

Coconut milk
Cod
Codfish
Coffee
Coix (seeds) YiYi Ren
Cola drink
Compote (fruits of the season)
Cooking oil
Coriander
Coriander (fresh)
Corn
Corn (fast polenta)
Corn (roasted)
Corn flour
Corn Grease (Polenta)
Corn silk tea
Corn starch
Cottage cheese
Couscous
Cow's milk (1.5% fat)
Crab
Cranberries
Cranberry
Cranberry
Cranberry jam
Cranberry juice
Cream sour 10%
Cream sour 20%
Creamer
Cress
Crispbread
Crucian
Cucumber
Cucumber (bitter)
Cucumber (spicy cucumber)
Cumin (Caraway seed)
Curcuma
Curd cheese 20%
Currant (black)
Currant (red)
Currant (white)
Currant jam (black)
Currant jam (red)
Currant juice (black)
Currants (black)
Currants (red)
Curry
Curry paste red
Daisy
Dandelion (young plants)
Dandelion juice
Dandelionroots tea
Dashi
Dates dried

Dates red
Deer meat
Deer meat
Deer's Bones
Deer's kidneys
Dill
Duck (heart)
Ducks egg
Dulse (seaweed)
Dyer's broom herb
Edam cheese
Eel
Eel smoked
Elderberries
Elderberry blossom tee
Endive salad
Evening primrose oil
Fennel
Fennel seeds ground
Fennel tea
Fenugreek (Trigonella foenum-graecum)
Fernet Branca (herbal bitter liqueur)
Feta cheese
Fig
Fig dried
Fish innards
Fish pieces mixed (fresh water)
Fish remains
Fish sauce
Flounder
Flower pollen
French beans
Fresh cheese
Fresh cheese from soya
Fresh cheese with herbs
Freshwater crab
Freshwater fish
Fructose (glucose)
Fruit mix juice
Fruit tea
Gail plum
Galangal
Garam Masala powder
Garlic
Gelatin white
Gelee Royal
Gentian root
Gentian root tea
Ginger fresh
Ginger oil
Ginger powder
Ginkgo fruit
Ginseng

Ginseng liqueur
Ginseng root
Goat
Goat and sheep's blood
Goat and sheep's brain
Goat and sheep's liver
Goat and sheep's milk
Goat and sheep's stomach
Goat cheese
Goose blood
Goose egg
Goose fat
Gooseberry
Gourd
Grape juice red
Grape juice white
Grapefruit (Pomelo)
Grapefruit dried peel
Grapefruit juice
Grapes red
Grapes white
Grapeseed oil
Grass carp
Green spelt
Green tea
Greengage
Ground
Ground caraway
Guava
Halibut (Flatfish)
Hawthorn
Herbal tea mix
Herbs bitter
Herbs of Provence
Herbs various
Herbs wild
Herring
Hibiscus tea
Hijiki
Hokkaido pumpkin
Honey
Honey wine (Met)
Hop
Horehound leaves
Horse meat
Hyssop
Iceberg lettuce
Jasmine blossoms tee
Jellyfish
Juniper berry
Kaki plum
Kalmus
Kefir
Kidney beans (red)

King Solomon's-seal
Kiwi
Kohlrabi
Kombu seaweed (Saccharina japonica)
Kukicha tea
Kumquats
Ladyfingers
Lamb bones
Lamb kidneys
Lamb liver
Lamb meat
Lamb shoulder
Lamb's lettuce
Lamb's lettuce
Lavender blossoms
Leaf salads (bitter)
Leek
Lemon
Lemon Balm (dried)
Lemon Balm (fresh)
Lemon juice
Lemon peel
Lemongrass
Lentils
Lentils black
Lentils red
Lentils yellow
Lettuce
Licorice root tea
Lima beans
Lime
Lime blossom tea
Linseed
Linseed (crushed)
Liver smoothing tea
Lobster
Longane
Loquate / Japanese medlar
Lotus roots
Lotus seeds
Lovage
Lovage seeds
Luo Han Guo fruit
Lychee
Lychee in Preserved
Lychee liqueur
Lye roll
Mallow (Malva sylvestris) blossom tea
Malt
Mango
Mango juice
Manioc flour
Mare's milk
Marjoram

Martini
Mayonnaise 50%
Mayonnaise 80%
Mediterranean fish (cod, plaice, haddock, sea eel, mackerel)
Medlar
Millet
Millet flakes
Mineral water
Mirabelle plum
Miso
Miso black (fermented)
Miso paste (soy bean paste)
Mixed Pickles
Mold cheese
Morel (black, dried)
Morel, dried
Mozzarella
Mu Erh Mushroom
Muesli
Mulberry fruit
Mulled Wine Spice
Mullet
Multi-grain bread (gray bread)
Mung bean
Mung bean sprouting
Mussels
Mustard
Mustard Dijon
Mustard medium hot
Mustard seeds
Mustard sweet
Mutton
Mutton
Nasturtium (nose-twister or nose-tweaker)
Nectarine
Nettles
Noodles (wheat) with egg
Noodles (wheat, lasagne) with egg
Noodles (wheat, ribbon noodles) with egg
Noodles (wheat, spaghetti) with egg
Noodles (whole grain) with egg
Nori, purple seaweed, red algae
Nutmeg
Oat
Oat flakes (whole grain)
Oat flakes roasted
Oat flour
Oat fusion (baby food)
Oat meal
Oat milk
Octopus

Octopus
Okra
Onion (shallot)
Onion (spring onion)
Onion read
Onion white
Orange
Orange blossom
Orange dried peel
Orange grated peel
Orange jam
Orange juice
Orange peel
Oregano dried
Oregano fresh
Oyster mushroom
Oyster shell powder
Oysters
Papaya
Parsley
Parsley root
Parsnip
Passion blossoms tea
Passion fruit
Peaches
Peaches (canned)
Peanut butter
Peanut oil
Pear
Pear juice
Pearl barley
Pearl barley
Peas
Peas, green
Pepper (ground)
Pepper Cayenne
Pepper powder (hot)
Pepper white (ground)
Peppercorns
Peppermint
Peppermint tea
Pepperoni
Pepperoni, red, pitted, halved
Pepperoni, yellow, pitted, halved
Peppers
Peppers (rose peppers)
Peppers (sweet)
Peppers powder
Perch
Pheasant
Pickle
Pig blood
Pigeon
Pigeon egg

Pimento
Pineapple
Pineapple (from a can)
Pineapple juice without sugar
Pinto beans speckled
Plaice
Plum
Plum dried
Plums
Pomegranate
Pork Bacon
Pork brain
Pork fat (lard)
Pork ham
Pork ham cooked
Pork ham smoked
Pork heart
Pork kidneys
Pork knuckle
Pork Lard
Pork liver
Pork lung
Pork marrow bones
Pork meat
Pork sausage (Bratwurst) Pork skin
Pork stomach
Pork/beef sausage (smoked)
Pork's intestine
Potato
Potato (mealy)
Potato flour
Prickly pear
Processed cheese 12%
processed cheese 30%
Prosecco
Psyllium seed
Pudding powder vanilla
Pumpernickel (dark bread)
Pumpkin
Quail
Quail egg
Quince
Quinoa
Rabbit
Rabbit (wild)
Rabbit liver
Rabbit meat
Radicchio
Radish
Radish (white, green, purple-red)
Radish black
Radish horseradish
Radish leaves
Raisins

Raspberry
Raspberry dried (immature)
Raspberry jam
Raspberry leaf tea
Red beet
Red berry (without sugar)
Red cabbage
Red wine
Reishi mushroom
Rhubarb
Ribworttea
Rice (fragrance)
Rice (Gaoliang / Sorghum)
Rice (whole grain)
Rice Basmati
Rice black
Rice flour
Rice long grain rice
Rice malt
Rice mash
Rice noodles
Rice red
Rice round grain
Rice starch
Rice sticky
Rice sweet
Rice variety any
Rice wild (nature rice)
Romaine lettuce / lettuce salad
Rose blossom tea
Rose hip
Rose hip tea
Rose leaf tea
Rosefish
Rosemary
Rucola
Rum
Rusk
Rye
Rye flour
Rye wholemeal bread
Safflower (Dyer's thistle / Hong Hua)
Saffron
Sage
Sago (cereals)
Sake
Salsify
Salt
Salt (herbal)
Sauerkraut (cutted cabbage fermented)
Savory
Savoy cabbage / kale
Sea buckthorn
Sea cucumber

Seacrab
Shark
Sheep's milk
Sheep's milk yoghurt
Sherry (whine)
Shiitake, dried
Shrimp
Shrimps
Skim milk powder
Slug
Sorrel
Sour cherries
Sour cream 15% fat
Sour milk
Sour milk cheese 20%
Sourdough
Soy flour
Soy noodles
Soy sauce
Soy Tofu
Soy Tofu smoked
Soya Cuisine (soy cream)
Soybean milk
Soybeans
Soybeans, black
Soybeans, blacks, fermented
Soybeans, yellow
Spelled (Dark) bread
Spelled flakes
Spelled grain
Spelled semolina
Spelled wholemeal flour
Spinach
Spiny lobsters
Spirit
Spurdog (spiny dogfish, Schillerlocken)
St. Benedict's thistle, blessed thistle,
holy thistle, spotted thistle
Star anise
Strawberries
Strawberry jam
Strawberry Juice
Sweet potato
Tabasco
Tangerine
Tarragon (Estragon)
Tea mixture uric acid lowering
Thistle oil
Thyme
Thyme dried
Toast bread (whole grain)
Tomato
Tomato dried
Tomato juice

Tomato paste
Tomato puree
Tonic Water
Topinambur
Trout
Trout (smoked)
Truffle
Tsampa (roasted barley flour)
Turkey breast meat
Turkey ham
Turmeric (yellow root)
Turnip
Turnips
Umeboshi paste
Umeboshi plums (Japanese apricots)
Valerian
Vanilla
Vanilla pod
Vanilla powder
Vanilla sugar natural
Vegetable juice
Vinegar (Apple vinegar)
Vinegar (Red wine vinegar)
Vinegar Aceto Balsamico
Vinegar Aceto Balsamico white
Wakame
Water
Water hot
Watermelon
Wax gourd
Wheat
Wheat beer
Wheat bran
Wheat bulgur
Wheat flakes
Wheat flatbread/pita bread

Wheat flour
Wheat flour whole grain
Wheat semolina
Wheat semolina for children
Wheat/Rye/Gray-black bread with yeast
Wheatgrass juice
Wheatgrass powder
Whey
White beans
White bread (baguette)
White bread (pretzel sticks)
White bread (roll)
White bread (wheat bread)
White breadcrumbs
White cabbage
White dumpling bread (wheat bread cut into chunks)
White wine
Whitefish
Whole grain bread
Wholemeal flour
Wild boar meat
Wild garlic (garlic spinach)
Wild herbs
Wild strawberries
Wormwood
Wormwood herb
Yam root, yam root tuber
Yarrow
Yarrow tea
Yeast
Yew nut
Yoghurt vanilla
Yogi tea
Yogurt (natural, 1.5% fat)
Zucchini

10.3 Use ingredients: little

-

10.4 Do not use contra-acting foods

Cola drink (low calorie)
Stevia (candyleaf, sweetleaf)

Sugar substitute (sweetener)

11 Herbs and their effects

11.1 Basil

It has a beneficial effect on flatulence and nausea, relaxing and soothing. Good to fight emphysema, bronchitis, whooping cough, high blood pressure, headache, mouth odor, warts, hiccup, gout, migraine.

11.2 Mugwort

Reduces bleeding, alleviates pain. In the kitchen, mugwort is used as a spice for fat food. Since it contains many bitter substances, it boosts fat burning and promotes digestion.

11.3 Savory

Stomach-strengthening, soothing and appetizing. Ideal for prevent colds, strengthens the immune system. In case of incontinence or nocturnal wetting (not for children), put the beans in liquor for libido.

11.4 Coriander

The essential oils are appetizing, digestive, cramping and soothing in stomach and intestinal disorders.

11.5 Herbs various

Appetizing, lots of trace elements and vitamins

11.6 Chives

Bactericide, prevents cancer, strengthens gastric juice production, promotes digestion and blood circulation, promotes growth, triggers stagnation.

11.7 Lovage

Stimulates digestion, reduces pain. Extracts of the root are used to flush out urinary tract infections and prevent kidney gravel.

11.8 Marjoram

Helps to digest fat foods, strengthens digestive organs, helps to fight colds, strengthens menstruation, promotes skin healing.

11.9 Oregano

It has an anti-digestive, calming and nerve-strengthening effect, helps to fight cramping stomach and intestinal disorders. The ingredient Carvacrol has an anti-inflammatory effect.

11.10 Parsley

Stimulates liver function, detoxifies. Forces urinating. Relieves flatulence. Digestive and menstrual stimulating, birth-accelerating, memory-enhancing, blood-purifying, skin-smoothing.

11.11 Rosemary

Promotes digestion, relieves bloating, strengthens lung, spleen and kidney. Affects the circulation and nerves. Appetizing. Baths help to fight circulatory disorders as well as with gout and rheumatism.

11.12 Sage

Good to fight yeast infections. The leaves have a digestive effect and are used in greasy foods. Antiperspirant effect. Helps to relieve coughing attacks. Dries out (TCM).

11.13 Black caraway

Detoxifying, immunoregulatory. In addition, the oil should stimulate the formation of bone marrow cells and generally protect body cells from viruses.

11.14 Thyme

Disinfecting. It stimulates the blood circulation, increases the appetite and helps to digest fat meat better. Strengthens lungs and spleen (TCM).

12 Basics of Nutrition

The basic principles of nutrition described herein are general recommendations. They are not aimed at a specific form of therapy. Recommendations concerning a therapy have priority.

12.1 Nutrition

Regular meals in a relaxed atmosphere. A warm breakfast is considered a good start into the day.

The main meals ought to be taken for lunch – supper in the early evening. Pay attention to feeling hungry or sated: don't eat too much nor remain hungry is the rule

Prepare the meals freshly from natural, regional products. Frozen, heat-conserved, industrially prepared or foodstuffs cooked in the microwave oven are rejected.

Choice of foodstuffs according to the season: more cooling food in summer, more warming food in winter.

Eat cooked food at least twice a day. Food and drinks ought to be lukewarm, never ice-cold or hot.

Raw vegetables, briefly cooked vegetables, freshly squeezed juices and mineral water are not recommended. Milk and dairy products are only included in the diet if they don't cause problems.

Don't use therapeutic recipes over a longer period without consulting your doctor or therapist.

Varied food

Enjoy the diversity of foodstuffs. Characteristics of a balanced nutrition are variety, suitable combination and a balanced quantity of rich and low energy foodstuffs (on one hand avoiding undersupply with essential nutrients and on the other hand to take to many undesirable substances).

A lot of Cereal Products - and Potatoes

Bread, pasta, rice, cereal flakes (best wholemeal) as well as potatoes contain almost no fat, but many vitamins, mineral nutrients, trace elements, roughage and secondary plant substances. These foodstuffs ought to be taken with low-fat side dishes.

Vegetables and Fruit – „Take Five" every day …

5 portions of vegetables and fruit a day, as fresh as possible, briefly cooked, or maybe one portion as a juice – ideal as a side dish to every meal as well as snack between meals: Thus a lot of vitamins, mineral nutrients as well as roughage and secondary plant substances

Daily milk and dairy products
Milk and Dairy Products every Day, once or twice per Week Fish;
meat, sausages as well as eggs moderately. These foodstuffs contain
valuable nutrients like calcium in the milk, iodine selenium and omega-3
fat acids in saltwater fish. Meat is favorable due to its high content of
disposable iron and the vitamins B1, B6 and B12. Quantities of 300 – 600
g meat and sausage per week are sufficient. Prefer low-fat products,
especially in meat- and dairy products.

Low-fat and fatty Foodstuffs
Fat supplies us with essential fat acids and fatty foodstuffs contain also
fat-soluble vitamins. Fat is high in energy; therefore much fat in the food
may cause overweight, possibly also cancer. Too many saturated fat
acids may further a tendency for cardio-vascular diseases in the long
term. Prefer vegetable oils and fats (e.g. rapeseed-, olive-, soya-oils and
solid fats produced therefrom). Beware of invisible fat in meat- and dairy
products, pastry and sweets as well as in fast-food and convenience
foods. 70 – 90 g fat per day is sufficient.

Moderately Sugar and Salt
Take sugar and foods/drinks containing various kinds of sugar (e.g.
glucose syrup) only occasionally. Use herbs and spices as well as a little
salt creatively. Prefer salt containing iodine.

Plenty of Liquids
Water is absolutely essential. Drink 1-2 l liquids every day. Prefer water
(with or without gas) and other low-calorie drinks. Alcoholic drinks should
not be taken.

Tasty Dishes, carefully cooked
Cook the meals with as low temperatures and as short as possible, using
little water and fat – this preserves the original taste, keeps the nutrients
intact and prevents the production of harmful compounds.

Take time and enjoy the food
Take your Time and enjoy your Food
Eating consciously helps to eat right. The eye enjoys food, too. It's fun,
invites to enjoy varied dishes and stimulates the feeling of satiety.

Watch your Weight and stay in Motion
A balanced diet and a lot of exercise and sport (30 – 60 min/day) are a
healthy combination. The right weight furthers well-being and health.
Thermals, directional effectiveness, digestive power

There are various criteria for judging the effectiveness of herbs and foodstuffs.

The use of certain herbs and ingredients is based on observations of the effects on the body which these foodstuffs, herbs and spices show after having eaten them. The medical science has developed following system: Every ingredient or herb has a directional effectiveness. Furthermore, there are herbs which have a special effect on certain organs.

The basic condition for a healthy metabolism is to obtain sufficient energy from food and that the digestive process doesn't use too much energy. An easily digestible meal makes content and sated, doesn't cause flatulence and fatigue after the meal. The perfect spices increase the healthiness of our meals. Very often, just small doses of herbs and spices will suffice. They are not used to make us sated, but to help our digestive organs to digest the food.

12.2 Recipes

The recipes list the ingredients to be used and the cooking instructions show how the dish is prepared. The list of ingredients shows the concerned quantities as well as the relevance for the therapy. If you find „less than mentioned", try to comply or find an alternative from the „list of recommended foodstuffs". Mostly it shall result just in a small change of taste when you simply avoid this ingredient.

Mild cooking methods: boiling, stewing, poaching, steaming
Strong cooking methods: barbecuing, roasting, frying, smoking
Balanced cooking methods: deep-frying, baking brick
Deep-freezing and warming in the microwave oven should be avoided (denaturalization).

12.3 Foodstuffs

Foodstuffs have an effect on body and soul like medicinal herbs, only a very much milder one. Dietary advice is mainly based on regional foodstuffs. The knowledge about the effects of each foodstuff and the knowledge, when which foodstuff shall be used, is based on the orthodoschool of medicine. Use ecologic-organic products, if possible. As everything should be cooked for a long time due to a better digestability and very rarely eaten raw, the food agrees with everyone.

The classification of the foodstuffs according to their effect on the body is the basis in order to achieve a harmonious status of health.

Dietary advisors do not recommend certain foodstuffs for everyone. The individual diet is tailor-made for the individual constitution.

Buy only fresh and ripe fruit and vegetables. You ought to leave unripe fruit and vegetables and such with brown spots and wilted leaves behind in the market. In this case take deep-frozen goods (never ready-to-serve dishes!). Fruit and vegetables are deep-frozen immediately after harvesting and often contain more vitamins and minerals than the goods from the vegetable shelf. Whereas conserved or tinned goods contain very much less biological substances. Also, salt, sugar and others are mostly added to the latter. Never leave the foodstuffs in the water after washing them to avoid that many vital substances get drowned. Clean salads, fruit and vegetables immediately before serving.

Please make sure of the hygienic processing of foodstuffs. Clean your salads, fruit and vegetables carefully. When cooking with meat, prepare all ingredients first and then process the meat products. Clean the worktop and tools very carefully. Wooden surfaces ought to be treated with a mild disinfectant regularly in order to reduce germination.

Store fruit and vegetables separately, if possible. Harvested fruit and vegetables are still alive and emit e.g. ethylene gas, which makes other products ripen and age faster. Keep meat and fish in the closed packaging or store them in the fridge in closed containers.

12.4 Herbs

There are some basic rules for storing medicinal herbs. On principle, herbs must be protected from direct sunlight, humidity and heat.

Containers for the storage of herbs may be glasses, ceramic jars and even plastic containers. However, plastic is a rather unsuitable material and should only be a short-term solution. In case of glass containers, use a dark material.

Medicinal herbs cannot be kept for any long period. The shelf life of herbs is limited. However, it can be prolonged with suitable storage. The place should be dark, rather cool and absolutely dry. A wooden medicine cabinet, placed not directly next to a source of heat, would be ideal. Never buy large quantities of herbs so as not to have to throw them away. Label the container with the name of the herb and the date of harvesting or processing.

13 Other dietic-books

The following syndromes of dietetics, TCM or for a therapy supplement for cancer are available.

Dietetics

E001. Nutrition of the infant - baby food
E002. Nutrition during lactation
E003. Nutrition in old age
E004. Nutrition of children and adolescents
E005. Nutrition of athletes
E006. Light weight
E007. Pregnancy
E008. Full food

Protein and electrolyte - kidneys
E009. (hemodialysis) dialysis treatment
E010. Acute renal failure
E011. Chronic renal insufficiency
E012. Nephrotic syndrome
E013. Kidney stones (nephrolithiasis)

Gastrointestinal tract - pancreas
E014. Acute pancreatitis (inflammation of the pancreas)
E015. Chronic pancreatitis (inflammation of the pancreas)

Gastrointestinal tract - small intestine and large intestine
E016. Acute obstipation (constipation)
E017. Chronic obstipation (constipation)
E018. Colon irritabile
E019. Diverticulitis
E020. Acquired lactose intolerance (lactose malabsorption)
E021. Fructose malabsorption
E022. Glutensensitive enteropathy (celiac disease)
E023. Colectomy
E024. Short Bowel Syndrome

Gastrointestinal tract - liver, gallbladder, bile ducts
E025. Acute and chronic hepatitis (inflammation of the liver)
E026. Cholelithiasis (bile stones)
E027. fatty liver
E028. cirrhosis

Gastrointestinal tract - Stomach and duodenal intestine
E029. Acute gastritis
E030. Chronic gastritis
E031. Stomach bleeding
E032. Ulcus ventriculi and duodenal ulcer
E033. Condition after gastric surgery

Gastrointestinal tract - oral cavity and esophagus
E034. Stomatitis
E035. Esophageal carcinoma (esophageal cancer)
E036. Refluosophagitis (heartburn)

Special diseases
E037. Phenylketonuria (PKU)
E038. Rheumatic joint diseases

Metabolism
E039. Obesity (overweight)
E040. Diabetes mellitus
E041. Eating disorders (underweight)

Fat metabolism
E042. Hypercholesterolaemia (increased cholesterol level)
E043. Hepatic Encephalopathy

Heart and circulation
E044. Arteriosclerosis (arterial calcification)
E045. Heart insufficiency
E046. Hypertension
E047. Hyperuricaemia and gout

Changed nutrient requirements
E048. In case of fever
E049. For malignant diseases
E050. After burns
E051. Radiation and chemotherapy

CANCER
E100. Pancreatic cancer
E101. Bladder cancer
E102. Blood cancer (leukemia)
E103. Breast cancer
E104. Colorectal cancer
E105. Gastric cancer
E106. Kidney cancer
E107. Esophageal cancer

TCM
E200. Bladder - moisture heat in the bladder
E201. Bladder - moisture and cold in the bladder
E202. Bladder - emptiness and cold in the bladder
E203. Large intestine - external cold affects the large intestine
E204. Large intestine - moisture heat in the large intestine
E205. Large intestine - heat blocks the intestine II acute
E206. Large intestine - dryness of the colon
E207. Large intestine - Yang deficiency (cold)
E208. Heart - Blood insufficiency
E209. Heart - Blood stagnation
E210. Heart - Fire
E211. Heart - Hot mucus clogs the heart pores

E212. Heart - Cold mucus clogs the heart pores
E213. Heart - Qi deficiency
E214. Heart - Yang deficiency
E215. Heart - Yin deficiency
E216. Liver - Ascending Liver Yang
E217. Liver - Blood deficiency
E218. Liver - Blood stagnation
E219. Liver - Moisture heat in liver and gall bladder
E220. Liver - Fire
E221. Liver - Gall bladder Qi-Empty
E222. Liver - Cold in the liver meridian
E223. Liver - Qi stagnation
E224. Liver - Wind
E225. Liver - Wind with ascending liver Yang
E226. Liver - Wind with blood anemic
E227. Liver - Wind with extreme heat
E228. Lung - Qi deficiency
E229. Lung - Mucus-moisture in the lungs
E230. Lung - Mucus-heat in the lungs
E231. Lung - Mucus-cold in the lungs
E232. Lung - Dryness of the lungs
E233. Lung - Wind-heat attacks the lungs
E234. Lung - Wind-cold affects the lungs
E235. Lung - Yin deficiency
E236. Stomach - Bloodstagnation
E237. Stomach - Fire
E238. Stomach - Cold with liquid
E239. Stomach - Nutrition stagnation
E240. Stomach - Qi deficiency
E241. Stomach - Rebellious Qi
E242. Stomach - Yin Emptiness
E243. Spleen - Heat and moisture attack the spleen
E244. Spleen - Coldness and moisture affects the spleen
E245. Spleen - Qi deficiency
E246. Spleen - Qi deficiency + Declining spleen Qi
E247. Spleen - Qi deficiency + spleen does not control the blood
E248. Spleen - Yang deficiency
E249. Kidney - Heart and kidney no longer communicate
E250. Kidney - Jing deficiency
E251. Kidney - Kidneys cannot receive the Qi
E252. Kidney - Qi is not stable
E253. Kidney - Yang deficiency
E254. Kidney - Yin deficiency

For further information visit di-book.com.